C000027782

Cooking Up Worship

A practical resource for creating simple but profound worship

David E Flavell

First published in 1999 by
KEVIN MAYHEW LTD
Buxhall
Stowmarket
Suffolk IP14 3DJ

© 1999 Kevin Mayhew Ltd

The right of David E. Flavell to be identified as the author
of this work has been asserted by him in accordance
with the Copyright, Designs and Patents Act 1988.

All rights reserved. No part of this publication may be
reproduced, stored in a retrieval system, or transmitted,
in any form or by any means, electronic, mechanical,
photocopying, recording or otherwise, without the prior
written permission of the publisher.

0 1 2 3 4 5 6 7 8 9

ISBN 1 84003 375 4
Catalogue No 1500275

Cover design by Jonathan Stroulger
Typesetting by Richard Weaver
Printed in Great Britain

Acknowledgements

I would like to thank several people who helped with the production of this book. Between them they have spent a considerable amount of time going through the manuscript and checking grammar, spelling and theological soundness. Each one has made a contribution to the finished document. As yet, not one of them has told me that I need to be *more* controversial, but I live in hope. Their names are:

> Jennifer Arthern, Mark Ashton, Stuart Clarke, Jane Cook, Chris Daniels, Marie Dove, Robert Eastaway, Neville & Pamela Flavell, Peter Grimwood, Jean Halden, Fiona Hewitt, Stephen & Gail Holliday, David MacDonald, Graham Slater, Kate Spall, Elaine Standish and Ross Tracy.

My most helpful critic is my wife Martha, who wasn't even my wife when this work was started. I dedicate this book to her, to thank her for her love, her support and her belief in me.

Rev David E Flavell
Liverpool
February 1999
http://dspace.dial.pipex.com/evo/index.htm

Thank you to The Savoy Hotel for permission to use the menu on page 26.

Cartoons are by kind permission of:

Randy Glasbergen
Dennis 'Max' Hengeveld
Dik Lapine

Every effort has been made to trace the owners of copyright material and we hope that no copyright has been infringed. Pardon is sought and apology made if the contrary be the case, and a correction will be made in any reprint of this book.

Board of fare

Worshippers of the world unite.
You have nothing to lose but your boredom!
DEF

Introduction

Congratulations on your purchase of *Cooking Up Worship*. I hope it will provide you with years of trouble-free service.

This book is written especially for new lay worship leaders, but its usefulness doesn't end there. Experienced laity and clergy will find much of vital interest, particularly those looking for a new approach that is both attractive *and* spiritually nourishing. Furthermore, there are suggestions for church leaders as to how they can 'grow' their own worship leaders.

A few years ago, the letters column of a national newspaper carried a discussion on sermons. Unfortunately for the preaching profession, one lady wrote in to say that she couldn't remember a single sermon she had heard in the last twenty years. This was cleverly answered by a man who replied that he could not remember a single meal that his wife had cooked in the last twenty years, but that he was sure that each one of them had been tasty, wholesome, nourishing and had done him good.

Cooking Up Worship takes this analogy further by comparing worship to a meal. What we share in church together should be interesting, wholesome, nourishing and do everyone good.

In recent years people have started to be more adventurous in the meals they prepare. Shelves are stacked with all kinds of cookbooks, enabling ordinary people to produce exciting meals. The idea of *this* book is to encourage ordinary people to produce exciting worship. You might never be as good at cooking as Delia Smith, but that shouldn't stop you from having a go. You might never be as good at leading worship as the Archbishop of Canterbury, but that shouldn't stop you from trying – and this book will help you.

Use the contents of this book as a resource, as an aid, as an encouragement and as a challenge to the established structures of the church. By following Jardin's Principle (see box on next page) you too will be able to produce simple but profound worship.

To worship is to give worth, to give glory to God. May this book help you to do just that.

Bon appetit!

Jardin's Principle

Jardin – who may have been a French Catholic, or a Scottish Presbyterian, nobody is quite sure – says that any given problem can be looked at in three ways:

(a) Simplistic (b) Complex (c) Simple but profound

Thus, for a restaurant, the aim can be stated in three ways, as follows:

(a) We should make more profit

(b) We should aim to increase our market share by three points in the next year, whilst concentrating on cutting capital input by one fifth, and also maximising menu efficiency and so on

(c) We should aim to give our customers what they really want.

Answer (a) is simplistic – of course we want to make more profit. Answer (b) is complex and will run to dozens of pages. Answer (c) is simple, but profound. It is a very easy concept to get across, but in another way it raises more questions than it answers. How do we give our customers what they really want? How do we find out? How do we deliver? How do we get everybody working in the restaurant to take responsibility for this? And there are many more questions like this.

But doesn't this ring a bell for Christians? Isn't there somebody we know who, when asked complex theological questions, came back with simple but profound answers which raised a whole new set of questions? It should come as no surprise to us that Jesus was a great Jardinist, long before the *Principle* was thought of.

Take Luke Chapter 10, the story of the Good Samaritan:

- The original question is 'Teacher, what must I do to inherit eternal life?'

- Jesus asks, 'What does the Law say?'

- To which the answer comes: 'Love the Lord your God with all your heart, and with all your soul, with all your strength and with all your mind; and your neighbour as yourself.'

- Jesus says, 'That is the right answer'.

Now the 'love your neighbour as yourself' bit is simple but profound. It's a very deep subject upon which many a sermon has been preached. Unfortunately, the lawyer takes it as being simplistic. After all, a lawyer's job is to make simple things complex. He tries for a more intricate answer. The response he gets is one of the greatest stories in literature, that of the Good Samaritan, which is at once simple but profound, and to which there is no answer. So Jesus leads the lawyer beyond the simplistic and the complicated and into the simple but profound.

When we look at worship today, we have not made the same step forward. The great argument at present is between choruses and hymns. One side says 'Choruses are puerile – the words are childish'. In other words choruses are too simplistic. The other side says 'Hymns are boring – they're too slow and the words are old-fashioned and incomprehensible'. In other words hymns are too complex.

The argument is stuck at the stage of simplistic worship versus complex worship. Neither is adequate. To make a difference to people, what we really need is to provide *simple but profound* worship. That is your task. May this book show you how.

Chapter 1

Laying the table ———

——— Setting the scene

Preparing an act of worship is like preparing a meal. Why ? Because:

- whatever you do, it will never be to everybody's taste
- you mix together various ingredients to make the whole
- good quality ingredients make for a good quality meal
- some ingredients blend better together than others
- some people will be the equivalent of militant vegans and will be offended if you include something they don't like
- some people are obsessive about etiquette and liable to go berserk if you don't do everything in what they consider to be the right order and the right way
- some people only like the sweet bits and aren't bothered about how nourishing the food is
- some people go from place to place sampling the products until they are satisfied
- some people enjoy complaining, no matter how good it is
- what really counts is not how clever you are, but how good it tastes
- the best cooks sometimes have disasters
- it's easier to eat than to cook

Maybe you can work out some more comparisons of your own!

What are we getting at the moment?

What the institutional church tends to offer is 'Sunday roast'. It is the same thing each week, with the same set courses, the same approach, the same structure. A prevailing attitude is that if people don't like this approach, then they jolly well ought to: 'It was good enough for the last century, so it's good enough now. If people don't come to church, then it's their own fault. We should be grateful for what we get, no matter how bad it is. For what we are about to receive, may the Lord *make* us truly thankful. What we offer is right. And if you don't like paternalism, then you don't know what's good for you, sonny.'

That's fine for the ever-diminishing bunch who like it, but what about the rest of us?

In the 'golden age' of yesteryear, the whole family sat down together and ate Sunday lunch in the traditional way. Mum would prepare a starter, a main course and a pudding followed by coffee. Dad and the kids would volunteer to wash up and afterwards everybody would sit down to talk or watch the film on TV while Dad fell asleep and snored loudly.

In the same way, at Sunday worship, the Church family would come together in the traditional manner. The minister would prepare the service with a nice word for the children, who would then go off to Sunday school. He would then read the Bible and give his sermon while Dad fell asleep and snored loudly until Mum prodded him. There would be nice hymns and a touching benediction. The congregation would express their thanks and go home to the traditional Sunday lunch.

This world has disappeared, but has the Church really noticed? Only a small minority of households sit down to Sunday roast today. Only a small minority of households come to church today. *These facts are linked.* Just as society has changed its eating habits, so it has changed its worship habits. Sunday is now a day just like Saturday.

Yet people still need to worship. The spiritual dimension has not vanished from life. The mainstream church is not providing the answer; there is a resistance to change for fear of 'upsetting somebody'.

Two examples of change

In the North East of England, in Easington Village, the traditional way of worship had led to just six elderly people meeting together on a Sunday. By changing the way of doing things and letting the people lead the worship, the average weekly attendance grew to over forty adults within six months.

On Merseyside, the Liverpool Central Hall closed in 1994 and was sold to property developers because it had only a handful of worshippers. In 1998 a new Church was started in the upper room of a pub in Liverpool city centre. The services were led by a team who used attractive and relevant ways of worshipping, and numbers rocketed. (See Chapter 10 for more details.)

Seven meals that Jesus shared

☺ Wedding at Cana
John 2:1-11

☺ Feeding of the Five Thousand
Mark 6:30-44

☺ Dinner with Simon the Pharisee
Luke 7:36-50

☺ Meal with Mary and Martha
Luke 10:38-42

☺ Tea with Zacchaeus
Luke 19:1-10

☺ The Last Supper
Mark 14:17-25

☺ Breakfast in Galilee
John 21:9-14

Spiritual hunger

There is a need for change because the nation is starving. If the Church is not feeding people's spiritual hunger, *then it ought to be*. There is still a need for simple but profound worship, and there are too many churches where that need is not being met. Too many leaders in the Church want the congregation to accept what they are given, rather than to learn to worship for themselves.

This is not what the Church is supposed to be about. The Church is better at being true to itself when it follows the way of Jesus. He put himself out for those who found the religion of the day hard to understand. He said that he had not come to call the righteous, but sinners. He went to the outcasts of society, and ate with them in *their* way, in *their* homes. The Church expects outsiders to learn the Church way of doing things before they can be accepted.

People should feel at home in church. They should be allowed to be themselves in church. Instead they have to pretend to enjoy what they are given.

What needs to be done?

There is no standard meal that everybody will eat this Sunday lunchtime. There does not have to be a standard form of worship that every church has to provide this Sunday. There are no 'norms' in worship, no objective standards that are laid down in Scripture. Instead, leaders of worship make their own choices.

They often choose the traditional way, because that seems to be the easiest. But the traditional way is not working for the vast majority of the population who do not come to church, and I would assert that it is not working for a large number of people who *do* come to church and come out of a sense of duty.

How many times do people leave church thinking, 'That was all very nice, but completely irrelevant to me'? *I'm afraid it is far too many times.*

How many people really enjoy the style of their worship every week and how many would like more variety, more quality, more choice?

There needs to be a complete change in attitude if the Church is to provide meaningful worship in today's world. The crucial thing is that people are fed. *How* they are fed is less important. There is no one 'correct' way to share a meal. Sometimes simple food with friends, where everybody helps themselves from the packet, is better than a meal at a sophisticated restaurant where you're not quite sure if you're following the right etiquette. Simple, informal worship can be far better than an elaborate service where nobody knows whether they are following the protocol or not.

The one thing that *is* essential for a meal is food. Without food there is no meal. With food, any kind of food, a meal can be prepared. Traditionalists will demand that lamb cannot be served without mint sauce. Formalists

Seven ways to intimidate dinner guests

- 😟 Give them lots of cutlery and expect them to know what to use and when

- 😟 Wear formal dress and stare at them when they don't

- 😟 Stand up and sit down unexpectedly for special toasts

- 😟 Assume they know all about a subject and talk about it for ages

- 😟 Give them a meal full of gristle and expect them to say they've enjoyed it

- 😟 Ignore them completely and talk to your other friends

- 😟 Ask them to bring their children with them and then complain when they make a noise

You wouldn't do that to your dinner guests. Would you?

Seven ways to intimidate worship guests

- 😟 Give them lots of books and expect them to know what to use and when

- 😟 Wear formal dress and stare at them when they don't

- 😟 Stand up and sit down unexpectedly for hymns, prayers and readings

- 😟 Assume they know all about a subject and give a sermon about it for ages

- 😟 Give them a service full of dreary hymns and expect them to say they've enjoyed it

- 😟 Ignore them completely and talk to your other friends

- 😟 Ask them to bring their children with them and then complain when they make a noise

The Church isn't like this at all. Is it?

will direct that the port must be passed to the left and that gentlemen shall be properly dressed. But what we think of as essentials are culturally conditioned. What we think of as normal, may only be normal to us. For instance, one third of the world eats with its fingers, one third eats with chopsticks and only one third eats with cutlery. But if you started eating a meal with your fingers at home in Britain, your mother would give you a lecture about your table manners.

The one element that *is* essential for Christian worship is Jesus Christ. He said, 'For where two or three are gathered together in my name, there am I in the midst of them' (Matthew 18:20). With his presence among us, we are able to worship. Traditionalists will demand that we cannot have hymns without an organ. Formalists will direct that there must be a pulpit and that gentlemen shall be properly dressed. But some people will be worshipping this day in a prison cell, with nothing but the presence of Jesus Christ. And that is still worship.

Our ideas of Christianity are dominated by our experience of Western churches. If you suddenly started singing like they do in the Armenian Church (which sounds to the uneducated ear like a sort of Middle-Eastern melodic wail), the choir director would suggest you didn't come back again. Different traditions have different ingredients of worship. Thus *no set of ingredients is objectively right or wrong*; it all depends on local tastes. The diverse nature of Christian worship is a strength, not a weakness.

- There can be worship without hymns.
- There can be worship without Bible readings.
- There can be worship without prayer.
- There can be worship without books.
- There can be worship without a sermon.
- There can be worship without a building.
- There can be worship without a minister.
- There can be worship without a collection.
- Christians can worship together in silence, in the middle of nowhere.

The traditional Sunday service is *not* the only way to worship.

What makes a good meal?

There are three things that make a good meal. The first is the company. The second is the taste of the food. The third is the nourishment provided.

Proverbs 15:17 says: 'Better a meal of vegetables where there is love than a fattened calf with hatred.' (NIV) All but the hungriest carnivore would agree. With the right people, even a bad meal can be an enjoyable experience. Part of the fun can be laughing at the food!

Psalm 119:103 says: 'How sweet are your words to my taste, sweeter than honey to my mouth!' (NIV) The taste of food *is* important. People have to eat to live, but eating is meant to be an enjoyable experience. God has given us the ability to appreciate good things; we should use it. The old puritan idea, that we should not enjoy anything at all, is wrong.

For those visiting for the first time, let me reassure you that the overhead projector usually works, the lady who waters the plants is on holiday, the lapel mike is never ordinarily misplaced . . .

Proverbs 3:7-8 says: 'Do not be wise in your own eyes; fear the Lord and shun evil. This will bring health to your body and nourishment to your bones.' (NIV) People need to be nourished by any meal that is provided for them. Taste alone will encourage them to eat, but the food needs to be full of vitamins and essential nutrients to benefit them. Some people would love to eat chocolate all day, when what would really do them good is roughage and vegetables. The secret of great cooking is to take food that is *good for you* and to turn it into food that you *want to eat*.

What makes good worship?

In the same way, there are three things that make good worship. The first is the company. The second is the 'taste' of the presentation. The third is the nourishment provided. And in that order.

With friends, even bad worship can be an enjoyable experience. Part of the fun can be talking about the service afterwards. A bad sermon *can* be more thought-provoking than a good one. The listeners soon cotton on to the fact that the preacher has lost the plot and they start thinking about how they could say things better. In effect, they are constructing their own sermons on the subject, which means that they will remember the subject matter far longer.

The 'taste' of the presentation is vitally important. People want worship to be an enjoyable experience, and so it should be. Unfortunately for preachers, the music is usually far more important to the congregation than the sermon. People will tolerate a lousy sermon if they can enjoy a good sing. People will not be uplifted nearly so much by an oratorical *tour de force* if the music is dreary.

People need to be nourished by worship. Good music alone will encourage them and uplift them, but the worship needs to be full of the nutrients people require for a healthy spiritual life. They would love to sing about resurrection all day, but they need to hear about the cross and suffering. A good worship leader can challenge people's lives and look at the most profound of subjects, while being fascinating at the same time. Unfortunately the church often manages to achieve the opposite and makes the life-changing good news of Jesus Christ seem about as appealing as school dinners.

What can be done about it?

When you prepare a meal for your friends, you have a lot of advantages. First of all, you choose the company. You don't have to invite those you don't like, nor those who may kick up a fuss. Secondly, you choose the timing – when you want people to come. Thirdly, you know your kitchen and are used to being there. Finally, it's your home, so what you say goes, and if people don't like it, they still have to do what you say.

Pity the poor worship leader who is far less fortunate. All sorts of people will come to the church. Some will be regulars who know what they like; some will be strangers who have not been for ages; even those who you do not like will come. There will be a wide variety of different tastes and preferences. The worship leader has to try to cater for them all.

The facilities may leave a lot to be desired. You may have chosen a complicated recipe involving piano, Bach and the massed choirs of Atlanta, Georgia, to discover that the organist can only play the white keys. In a perfect world so much more could be done; in the real world there are limitations.

But this is not a cause for despair; there is hope, because you do control some things. Different cooks have different approaches and so can you. Just as everyone can cook something, especially if they are taught how, so *everyone can lead worship*. Some will do it better than others, but everyone has a part to play. Even if you have never done anything like it before, you too can be a cook in the kitchen of worship. Even if you have been cooking up worship for years, you too can use new recipes. Even if your church has been stuck in the same rut for years, you can encourage worship leaders to come forward.

In fact the real test of a chef is not whether, given the combined resources of the Savoy Hotel kitchens, they can come up with a masterpiece, but whether they can make anything half decent out of some rice, two onions and a tomato. Similarly, the real test of a preacher is not whether they can produce a brilliant sermon after the King's College Cambridge choir have performed, but whether they can hold together a service with no music and a congregation of just three people, one of whom is asleep, one of whom is reading the hymnbook and one of whom is having a terminal coughing fit.

There will be some star cooks, who make everything look easy and can make a banquet out of nothing. There are brilliant leaders of worship who can be simple yet profound in the most trying of circumstances. The link between them and you is that, a long time ago, they started where you are now.

So who can lead worship?

Anybody can worship; anybody can lead worship and lead worship well. God enjoys our worship *despite* what it sounds like. The sound of a prize-winning organist is as nothing compared to what the one who invented music can produce. Some people think God prefers classical music to pop, and traditional to modern, but whatever songs we sing, there must be tens of thousands of angels who could sing them more sweetly. God doesn't *need* our worship, but God does accept and enjoy it.

Mothers and fathers going to listen to the school orchestra are not bothered that it does not sound like the Berlin Philharmonic. In reality it may sound like the Berlin Zoo. Parents are interested that it is their children playing. 'Look, that's my David playing the

Two men went up to the temple to pray, one a Pharisee and the other a tax collector. The Pharisee stood up and prayed about himself: 'God, I thank you that I am not like other men – robbers, evil-doers, adulterers – or even like this tax collector. I fast twice a week and give a tenth of all I get.'

But the tax collector stood at a distance. He would not even look up to heaven, but beat his breast and said, 'God, have mercy on me, a sinner'.

I tell you that this man, rather than the other, went home justified before God. For everyone who exalts himself will be humbled, and he who humbles himself will be exalted (Luke 18:10-14 NIV).

Are you a Pharisee or a tax collector?

You might be a modern-day Pharisee if you:

☹ Look down on choruses as mindless.

☹ Look down on people who eat at McDonalds.

☹ Look down on people who like pop music.

☹ Look down on people who watch soap operas.

☹ Look down on people who read tabloids.

☹ Look down on people who wear the 'wrong' clothes.

☹ Can't cope with emotion in church.

You don't have to like burgers, pop music, soap operas or tabloid newspapers, but you shouldn't consider yourself a superior Christian to those who do.

Score:

2 or less out of 7 – You're doing okay.

3 out of 7 – You're on the way.

5 out of 7 – You need to change.

7 out of 7 – You are that Pharisee!

triangle at the back!' They are not so much interested in the music, they are interested in the children.

In the same way, God is not bothered that our singing is not always in tune; he's more interested that it's his children worshipping. 'That's my David worshipping there. Can you see him? That's my child and I delight in him.' God delights in our worship.

Psalm 149:4 says: 'For the Lord takes delight in his people; he crowns the humble with salvation.' (NIV) God is not interested in the worship, he is interested in his children.

In Old Testament days, people thought that God was fed by a sacrifice. They ritually killed and burned an animal in the hope that this would make God happy. They had special rules so that only the finest and purest would be offered to God. But this was not what God wanted.

Hosea 6:6 says: 'I want your constant love, not your animal sacrifices. I would rather have my people know me than burn offerings to me.' (Good News Bible)

God is not impressed with even the most skilful worship, but with the humility of our hearts and our readiness to be merciful. And that is why God is so angry if anyone places a stumbling block in front of one of his children by saying, 'You are not good enough to worship here'. Each one of us is only here by the grace of God. We are all like members of the school orchestra, desperately trying to hit the right note. Those of us who think we are good enough to play for the Berlin Philharmonic have missed the point entirely.

Another way of looking at worship is illustrated by the story of the little boy who asked his dad whether he wanted a drink. Well, the dad didn't really, but he said, 'Go on then, if you'd like to make me one'. The little boy was really happy to be helping his dad, so he got a glass and filled it with water and spilt a bit, and put his muddy thumb in it and nearly dropped it, before bringing it triumphantly to his father. 'There you are, Dad', he said. His father looked down at the dirty glass with muddy water in it and instead of throwing it away, he drank it straight down and said, 'Thank you, son, that was just what I needed', and the little boy beamed from ear to ear. That is just how it is with our worship. God does not need it; others could do it far better, but he accepts our worship, just because it is us and because he delights in us.

So be encouraged; God accepts our worship. But be challenged; work as hard on your worship as children do in rehearsing for the school orchestra. Pray as if everything depends upon God. Work as if everything depends on you. It is not only the important people to whom God listens; quite the opposite.

Not all stars

Not all Christians are good speakers, or have pleasing voices, or great intellects or even pleasant personalities. But worship is not about these things. If worship were about pleasant voices, then we would play tapes of Sir Lawrence Olivier (see Chapter 8). If worship were about intellectualism, we would read from Aristotle and not the Bible (see Chapter 4). If worship were about pleasant personalities, it would be led by chat-show hosts. But worship is about God. And God can use the least of his children in worship. To say that God cannot, is to question the power of God.

Worship does not have to be complicated and intellectual. Everybody in your congregation is capable of leading worship. Think right now of one person who you could encourage to start by giving them a copy of this book.

You can lead worship. *You* are good enough, because God accepts you. So how do you start? The next chapter, *Selecting the menu,* explains how.

Sunday Menu

Tomato soup

Roast beef and Yorkshire pudding

Apple pie

Time for a change?

Sunday Menu

The preacher chooses

The preacher leads

The people like it

or lump it

Time for a change?

Chapter 2

Selecting the menu ——————

—————— What goes into the service?

How do you go about choosing the menu? What elements must you include? That depends on three factors.

- The first factor is the people.
- The second factor is the venue.
- The third factor is the occasion.

The number of people to be fed and their dietary needs are important. The place in which you are eating and cooking makes a difference. The occasion may demand a special meal. The same factors can affect worship. For the moment, suppose that you are in your usual venue on an ordinary Sunday. The problem is that you can never tell exactly who will be there at worship. There may be regulars who are absent. There may be new people who just walk in off the street. People may have friends visiting. The numbers may be different from what you expect. You can *never assume anything* about the people coming to worship.

This is not very helpful. If you are preparing a meal and you have no way of knowing how many guests are coming, and what sort of things they like, you are in an impossible position. If you are preparing worship and you have no idea about the congregation attending and what sort of things they like, you have got a problem. You have to make some decisions. Perhaps it would be better to say you must always

be aware of the assumptions you are making about the people coming to worship.

Typically, too much tends to be taken for granted, either consciously or subconsciously. You take for granted a certain level of education; that people know their Bibles; that people know what they are doing; that people know what *you* are doing; that people can hear properly, and that the people who can hear are still listening.

If you use hymnbooks, you are expecting everyone to be both sighted and literate. If you ask people to rise from their seats, you are expecting that they can stand. If you send round a collection plate, you are expecting that folk have brought money with them.

However, the biggest and most dangerous presumption of all is that the congregation is just like you. You think to yourself, 'This is a good hymn; the congregation will like this'. If you are not careful, however, what you are really thinking is, 'This is a good hymn, *I* like it'. It is hard to avoid this because there is no way of knowing what other people are really thinking. Many a minister has been encouraged to hear someone say the words, 'Nice service, Vicar', only for them never to darken the door again.

You *should* tell the worship leader what you enjoyed and what you did not enjoy (in a loving manner). Feedback makes for good worship. If your leaders and preachers do not think they need any, you can always buy them a copy of this book as a Christmas present!

> # Never ASSUME anything, because it makes an ASS out of U and ME

One way round the problem of not knowing your congregation's intimate thoughts is to decide at what *sort* of people you are going to aim your service. If you do not consciously create a target audience, then the chances are that you will be aiming subconsciously at yourself. Here are three good questions to ask about everything you are proposing to do:

1. How would this sound to a regular churchgoer?

2. How would this sound to a new Christian?

3. How would this sound to an outsider?

If you think you can appeal to all three groups at once, then you are doing the right thing. It is much easier to appeal to Group 1, especially if you belong to Group 1. But if your church is on the move, you will want lots of people from Groups 2 and 3. Many churches would love to have ten new people through their doors each week. Embarrassment can occur when you assume there will only be Group 1, and Group 3 turns up.

The Toxteth Church held their Maundy Thursday service, which I was leading. I had prepared a traditional sermon for the six people I had envisaged coming, on the text 'He was a man of sorrows, and familiar with suffering'.

Immediately before the service started, the Youth Club next door announced that their end-of-term party was postponed from 7pm to 7.30pm, and would the children kindly wait outside in a peaceful and attentive manner.

They didn't – they came to us instead.

I had to change my tune very quickly, and instead of Plan A, we told the Easter story by question and answer instead. We went through the arrest, trial, crucifixion, burial and resurrection, in great detail.

To the question, 'So what do Christians eat on Maundy Thursday?' came back the answer, 'Butties and wine'. Then one of the children said a prayer, which we all had to copy, with our eyes shut and our hands together. Rather than finishing with 'Amen', it came to a halt with 'That's all'.

After half an hour, they left for the party, and I reverted to my original sermon, hymns and communion.

We've missed the point, if we think that God enjoyed one half of that service more than the other.

To include all three groups, you have to make a conscious effort. Don't aim to be smart, so that only the cleverest people will enjoy the worship and the rest will miss out. Instead, get your message across simply and sensitively

Self-indulgence

As a cook, you want to provide a meal that is both nutritious and tasty. You want to make something that people will enjoy, and yet find satisfying and nourishing. The way you do this is to think what sort of people will be dining, and then to provide what you think is suitable for them. You may be right, you may be wrong, but at least you've tried.

What would be unhelpful is to say 'I like baked beans, therefore everybody else likes baked beans, and if they don't there is something wrong with them'. Very few cooks would work in that way, but it's surprising how many leaders of worship do.

If you're leading worship as an opportunity to fulfil your own tastes in music and prayer, then you're failing the people. Self-indulgence has no part in worship.

and yet with depth for those who can appreciate it. This involves taking the time to explain what is going on, without being patronising, so that outsiders will feel comfortable and understand what is happening. On the other hand, it means that you don't avoid difficult Bible passages or hymns, just because they are difficult. The Gospel is simple enough to be understood by a child and yet deep enough for scholars to earn their living studying it. Your worship should be inclusive, so that everybody present can take part. Your aim is to be simple and profound at the same time.

If children are present, then you will need to work in a special way. For a discussion on how to include the children in worship, see Chapter 9.

Which items should I include?

The rest of this book is full of suggestions. Just as in preparing a meal, there are two decisions to make. The first decision is, 'Which courses should you include?' and the second is, 'Which recipes should you use?'

The first course is the *starter*, or in our case, the prayers. Just as a starter whets our appetite and tells our stomach that more food is coming, so the prayers put us in the right frame of mind to worship. Different recipes for prayer will be found in **Chapter 3**. It would be unusual to have no prayers at all in a service.

Chapter 4 looks at the Bible and the sermon, the *main course*. The Bible is at the heart of what takes place, and it would be very unusual to have no Bible readings at all in a service. But which ones are you to choose?

In **Chapter 5** we consider the hymns, the *pudding*. You do not always have to have a pudding, especially if the other courses are particularly filling. However, most people remember the taste of the pudding long after the other flavours are forgotten, and people tend to remember the hymns long after the sermon!

Chapter 6 looks in detail at all the different *side dishes* you can add to the meal:

- ☺ Family time
- ☺ Testimony
- ☺ Poetry
- ☺ Meditation

- ☺ Dance
- ☺ Offering
- ☺ Drama
- ☺ Ministry
- ☺ Video

In **Chapter 7** we look at special set meals, the special services of the church. You would not normally be expected to take these as they are reserved for the clergy in most churches. However, they are worth looking at in case you do get the opportunity.

Chapter 8 looks at practical tips for getting started.

Chapter 9 looks at children's menus.

Chapter 10 gives two case studies.

Chapter 11 asks 'What happens next'?

Chapter 12 offers resources and ideas.

Does there need to be a common theme?

Absolutely not. In the old days, the rule was white wine with fish and chicken, red wine with beef and lamb. Now the advice is: drink the wine you like! You are no longer tied to arbitrary rules.

Nor does there need to be a common theme in worship. This is one of the biggest mistakes made by the church of today. Worship leaders are putting a great deal of effort into matching their hymns and their readings and their prayers when this is completely unnecessary. What they should be doing is choosing singable

Inspector Morse

Inspector Morse is a character created by the crime writer Colin Dexter. In the television series of the same name, John Thaw plays the policeman who solves murders in the City of Oxford, which provides a beautiful backdrop.

One of the really clever features of the series is the incidental music. Often the name of the murderer is spelt out in Morse code as part of the background sounds.

The vast majority of people don't know Morse code so they miss out on this clever link. Fortunately, the basic story lines are so strong that this doesn't matter. If they never gave the name of the murderer *except* in Morse code, then there would be a lot of frustrated viewers out there.

When leading worship, make sure your basic story line is strong enough to be clear to everybody. Don't rely on clever links that people won't be able to pick up unless they have specialist knowledge. You may be very clever and perhaps a couple of people will appreciate your skill, but you want to communicate to everybody.

Beware the worship leader who condescendingly says, 'I don't know why I bother. There was only one person here today who really understood what I was saying. There's something wrong with *them*.'

hymns, understandable readings and straightforward prayers, because it doesn't matter whether everything goes together.

When I was training to be a preacher, I was told that the aim of the sermon was to link together the three given readings. Now a sermon could make those links to perfection in itself, and yet leave its listeners cold. Or a sermon could be based on just one of those readings – forget the other two, make one point, simply and forcefully.

As long as the courses are good, it doesn't matter what they are, or how they link together. If you are making a meal, then there are no hard and fast rules as to how one course follows another. It depends entirely on the way things are done locally. When you are putting together worship, there are no hard and fast rules as to how one item follows another. It depends on the way things are done locally.

The aim of a service is to worship God, not to match everything up beautifully. Few people notice whether your hymns go together. Few people notice whether your readings go together. Few people notice whether your prayers go together. Most people notice when they cannot sing the hymns and when they cannot understand the prayers.

When you are preparing the service, start from where the people are now. Don't be insensitive to their needs. Indulge your congregations by giving them what *they* want, because if you are not indulging them, you will be indulging yourself, and self-indulgence should have no part in worship.

Each part of worship should be good enough to stand by itself. There is no benefit in linking everything together, if you have to use weak material to do it.

Fish and chips do not have to be followed by sponge pudding. Coq au vin does not have to be followed by crème caramel. Lasagne does not have to be followed by tiramisu. You can mix and match different national dishes if you want. A meal *can* have a theme, but it is not compulsory. In the same way, worship can have a theme running through, but it is not mandatory.

Instead, construct your worship so that it is entertaining. You can challenge the congregation over their lack of faith, their lack of hope and their lack of love. You can tear them off a strip for their complacency. You can make them squirm in their seats for their sinfulness. You can portray the agony of the cross. But for God's sake, don't be dreary.

Seasonal themes

There are times of the year when a unified theme *can* be helpful. At Christmas or Easter or Harvest Festival, people like to sing the old songs. You can have what you want for Christmas dinner, but there's bound to be somebody disappointed if there isn't any turkey, and you can have what you want in a Christmas service, but there's bound to be somebody disappointed if you don't have *While shepherds watched . . .* Altogether now . . .

The problem with much of our worship today is not that it does not fit together cleverly, but that it is boring. And that is heretical, because Jesus was never boring. Jesus taught his disciples hard things. He told them about suffering. He turned over the tables in the Temple. He pointed out the hypocrisy of the Pharisees. His parables are not always comfortable, but they are always interesting and they are based on accessible everyday life situations.

The crowds came to listen to him, not because he was worthy, but because he had something worth saying. They were amazed that he spoke with authority, unlike the other religious leaders. He told simple stories, but they were profound. Dare we say that the Scribes and the Pharisees were complicated and boring? Jesus did not tell boring stories. Make sure you don't have boring services. Worship does not always have to be happy – it can be sad, it can be angry, it can be passionate, but it must not be dull. Make sure you have something worth saying.

A restaurant can serve meals of all different kinds. The food can be nutritious or full of fat. But, unless the food is tasty, it won't matter how good it is,

people will stop coming. There is no benefit in nutritious food if it remains uneaten.

A church can provide services of all different kinds. The worship may be deep and meaningful, or superficial. But unless the worship is entertaining and exciting, it does not matter how good it is, people will stop coming. There is no benefit in turgid, but well-meaning worship.

Ideally your worship should be both entertaining *and* nourishing. Worship should be inspiring, moving, thought-provoking, life-enhancing, heart-stirring, attitude-challenging, soul-enriching and Holy Spirit-filled. It should bring glory to God. This is far more important than whether it all fits neatly together with the same theme.

A good cook can take truly nourishing food and make it taste truly delicious – like ice cream! If you can do that with worship, then you will be able to get your congregations to swallow the hardest sayings in the Bible, and to do something about them.

Work at both aspects of your service. The following chapters will help you choose the right ingredients.

Menu

Starters

Tomato and mozzarella salad with pesto and tapenade
Panfried scallops with an orange and roast chilli oil dressing
Gamekeepers' broth with herb dumplings

Main dishes

Vegetable and mushroom lasagne with caraway butter sauce
Honey-roast salmon with bok choy, Asian pesto and diced mango
Grilled monkfish with oven-roasted tomatoes and shitake
mushrooms, topped with long beans and pancetta

Desserts and Cheese

Cappuccino brûlée
Banana and lime tart with hot fudge sauce
Selection of blue Stilton, Keen's Cheddar or Bonchester
with olive break

This is a genuine menu from *Upstairs*, one of the restaurants in the world-famous Savoy Hotel, London. There are dishes from at least four nations. The only theme is that they all sound wonderful!

Chapter 3

The starter

The prayers

A non-Christian friend told me that, in his opinion, prayers are like broad beans; you know they're good for you, but you don't enjoy them and you're glad when they're finished!

However, prayers should be like the starter to a meal. Ideally, the starter whets the appetite without filling the stomach. It should set the tastebuds tingling and tell the body that a meal is on the way. The prayers ready the soul for nourishment. They mark the change from talking to each other to listening to God. Prayers prepare you for worship together.

Richard Hannay's Thirty-Nine Articles

'It is a thing plainly repugnant to the Word of God, and the custom of the Primitive Church to have publick Prayer in the Church or to minister the Sacraments in a tongue not understanded of the people.' *Article Twenty-Four of the Thirty-Nine Articles of the Church of England (1563).*

In today's English you might say, 'There's no point praying, if the people can't understand what you're saying'. That means you have to pray loudly, clearly and in a language the people understand.

Seven famous prayers

☺ Father, forgive them for they know not what they do. *Jesus*

☺ God help me. *Anon*

☺ For what we are about to receive may the Lord make us truly thankful. *Anon*

☺ God, give us grace to accept with serenity the things that cannot be changed, courage to change the things that should be changed, and the wisdom to distinguish one from the other. *Reinhold Niebuhr*

☺ Jesus, Son of God, have mercy on me a sinner. *Orthodox Tradition*

☺ Lord, make me an instrument of your peace. Where there is hatred, let me sow love; where there is injury, pardon; where there is doubt, faith; where there is despair, hope; where there is darkness, light; where there is sadness, joy. O divine Master, grant that I may not so much seek to be consoled as to console, to be understood as to understand, to be loved as to love. For it is in giving that we receive; it is in pardoning that we are pardoned; it is in dying that we are born to eternal life. *St Francis of Assisi*

☺ Now I lay me down to sleep
I pray the Lord my soul to keep.
Should I die before I wake
I pray the Lord my soul to take.
Anon

Article Twenty-Four was written to stop the church using Latin in its services, but a 'tongue not understanded of the people' need not be a foreign language. It could be the English of yesterday. It could be the 'holy words' that only the chosen few initiates know. Dare I say it *could* be the words used every Sunday?

Understanding

There are three things to consider when leading public prayer.

- Does God understand your prayers?
- Do you understand your prayers?
- Do the people understand your prayers?

This may seem a little daunting, but it boils down to just the last question.

God understands your prayers even when you do not. Romans 8:26b says, 'We do not know what we ought to pray for, but the Spirit himself intercedes for us with groans that words cannot express.' (NIV) When you cannot put the words together, the Spirit helps.

God is not swayed by the eloquence of your prayers. 'God, help me by the benevolence of thy mercies' does not get a better hearing in heaven than 'God, help me'.

Jesus said in Matthew 6:7-8: 'And when you pray, do not keep on babbling like pagans, for they think they will be heard because of their many words. Do not be like them, for your Father knows what you need before you ask him.' (NIV)

So, if your heavenly Father knows what you need before you ask him, why bother to pray? There are several books on this subject, but there are three short answers. First of all, because it is good for you in that it helps you to try to understand the will of God; secondly, because it 'works', in that prayer does change things; and thirdly, because it gives God pleasure when you say out loud how you feel about your heavenly Father and express your needs to him. God doesn't *need* your praises, in the sense that you would make him resentful without them, but he does *delight in* your praises, just because they come from his children. Prayer changes the world, and prayer changes people, because God intervenes in the world today. God answers prayers, although not always in a way that suits everyone. (See the box.)

God always understands your prayers, no matter how mixed-up you get. He understands your language, your motives, even the things you don't say. It seems reasonable to assume that *you* understand your own prayers (and if you don't, then maybe you should).

That leaves the congregation. A good prayer is one that people understand. A bad prayer is one that people do not understand. Your prayers are *to* God, but your prayers are *for* your people. God can understand, however you say your prayers, even if they are in Latin. But if you start reciting Latin prayers out loud, most of your listeners will not be able to understand them.

If you go on too long people will stop concentrating. The textbook answer to the question, 'Can you have

A dog's prayer

When Tara, my dog, had to go for a minor operation, the vet told me that she mustn't be allowed to have anything to eat the night before.

When feeding time came, there was no food in her bowl, so she came to see me, to find out what was going on. I told her that she couldn't have any food and she went away to think about it. She came back and tried to attract my attention. Still the answer was 'no', so she went and hid under the bed thinking she must have done something wrong and was being punished. Then she got angry and barked at me. Still there was no food. Finally she went and sulked, and seemed to wonder whether I still loved her. I could have explained the situation until I was blue in the face, but she would never have been able to understand. The next day she had her operation and all was well. Now she eats as normal.

When we are suffering, we go through the same process of surprise, worry, guilt, fear, anger and doubt. We pray to God, but don't get the answer we want, and wonder whether God still loves us, and why there is no explanation for our pain. And yet, even if God explained until he was blue in the face, we couldn't understand.

Tara had to trust her master, even when life didn't make sense. We have to trust our Master, even when our lives don't make any sense. God hears our prayers and knows what we need. God will give us what is best for us.

too much prayer?' is 'No, you can't'. That's very pious. But Jesus was rarely pious. He said, 'Don't gush like the pagans do. They think lots of words make a difference. But they don't'. If the prayers are the starter for the meal of worship, then you don't want too many, otherwise people will be full before the main course arrives. In my experience, anything more than two minutes of prayer without a gap or response, will send people drifting off, thinking about whether they've left the gas on. Several short prayers with breaks are better than one over-long prayer. The starter should whet the appetite, not fill the stomach. Simple and profound prayers are better than complicated prayers.

Praying to whom?

Purists would say that you pray *to* God the Father, *through* Jesus the Son, *with* the help of the Holy Spirit. But you can pray to God the Father, or God the Son, or God the Holy Spirit (or all three, by praying to the Trinity). Don't worry about getting it wrong; even if you start off praying to Jesus and end up praying to God the Father, your prayers are heard. It's easy to get mixed up. And it is better to pray to God in a mixed-up way than never to approach God at all.

The question of praying to saints and in particular Mary, the mother of Jesus, is one that divides different denominations. The Catholic Church believes that Mary and the saints are very much alive and able to speak on our behalf to God when we pray to them. Protestants believe that we should go to God directly through Jesus. It would be very unusual to pray to a saint in Protestant worship. You should be sensitive to the traditions of the people who will be present.

What kind of prayers?

There are lots of different sorts of prayers and lots of ways of praying. You can choose any you like, as there are no set rules. The options, when praying, are to use your own prayers or to use somebody else's. Both are fine.

Many people use books of prayers from which they choose material (Chapter 12 has some suggestions). This is a good way to start. You should always read the prayer through before-hand to see if it contains difficult words, or anything with which you might disagree. Choose prayers that are good in themselves. Prayers do not have more value because they were written by somebody famous, or by a person who lived a long time ago. Thousand-year-old recipes may have withstood the test of time, but on the other hand they may be stale. If the authors of these prayers or recipes were alive today they might write something totally different.

Your own prayers are fine, too. If you feel nervous about praying in public, then a good tip is to write down prayers the night before. You can be an individual without having to be spontaneous. If you were cooking an impor-

tant meal and wanted everything to be home-made, it would make sense to prepare as much as you could the night before. Prayers do not have more value because you make them up on the spot. Remember, the quality of prayers depends not on their grammatical correctness but on the way they're received by people.

When you make up your own prayers you can use whatever words you like. God hears all your prayers. You do not have to use a special language or religious words. There is no need for excessive formality, but neither is there a place for being flippant. You should speak to God as you would speak to your earthly father, with love, with respect and with warmth. You do not have to use 'thee' and 'thou' unless you want to. Few people (unless they come from Sheffield, like me) say 'thee' and 'thou' in ordinary speech these days. However, you can safely assume that most people know what the words mean, even if they consider them to be old-fashioned. (See the box.)

Use vocabulary you feel comfortable with, or more importantly, that the people will feel comfortable with. Don't worry too much about grammar or syntax. Don't use long words when short ones will do. Keep it simple. Make your words appropriate for the people you will be leading in prayer. God hears prayers even when the subject doesn't agree with the verb. Aim for clarity, not technical proficiency. Speak the words of the marketplace, the playground and the office, not the words of the church.

Nah den dee*

Originally 'thee' and 'thou' were not terms of awe, but terms of intimacy. 'Thou' is just the singular form of 'you', just as in French, 'tu' is the singular and familiar form of 'vous'. A French person would say 'tu' to a child or a loved one, but a more formal 'vous' to a colleague or a boss. The Lord's Prayer in French calls God 'tu', which suggests that God is a loved one rather than a boss. Why not let your prayers be like that? In English, you can call God 'thou' or 'you', whichever you prefer. There is no right or wrong way. Use the language of the people.

*Nah den dee comes from 'Now then, thee' and means 'Hello, how are you?' in Sheffield.

Subject

So what should you pray about? That's up to you. Some people have complicated ways of remembering so that they get their prayers in just the 'right' order. For instance, they remember the word ACTS, which stands for

- ☺ Adoration
- ☺ Confession
- ☺ Thanksgiving
- ☺ Supplication

Prayer experts start off with *Adoration* where they praise God for who God is. Then they make their *Confession* where they say sorry to God for what they have done or failed to do. Next comes *Thanksgiving* when they thank God for the many things they have been given, above all for the gift of Jesus. Finally comes *Supplication* where they ask for God's help in our needy world.

The Bible is full of prayers which cover all these subjects, in particular the Psalms:

- ☺ Psalm 9 – I will praise you, Lord, with my whole heart
- ☺ Psalm 51 – Have mercy upon me, O God
- ☺ Psalm 107 – Give thanks to the Lord
- ☺ Psalm 121 – I will lift my eyes to the hills. Where is my help?

This is all very well, but you don't have to know *all* the fancy words to be able to pray. Just pray about your concerns and the concerns of the people. There are always things to give thanks for, even when all that can be said is, 'Thank you, God, that life isn't usually like this'. There are always things to say sorry for, even when you are feeling particularly virtuous. There are always needs in the world, for peace, for reconciliation and for healing. God does not mind in what order you pray and what words you use just as long as you pray.

When you pray in public, you are leading people in prayer and expressing on their behalf what they all want to bring before God. God knows the hearts of everyone there, and he does not need your help to do that. *But the people do need your help.* Some find it hard to pray. They do not always know the words. They cannot express themselves easily. They feel inadequate. They worry that everyone else in church knows how to pray properly except them.

You can help by putting *their* thoughts into *your* words. This is not a question of language, or education, or knowledge; it is the ability to put yourself in somebody else's shoes and speak on their behalf. The people who pray best are not those with the education, but those with an instinctive feeling for the needs of others. Ideally, your prayers should be of the people, by the people and for the people. You should be saying what people are thinking.

Making claims

Prayers in public are not the same as your own private prayers spoken out loud. You have to think of others besides yourself. You should try to include everybody in your prayers. Don't push people out. It is fine to say, 'God, we're glad to be here this morning', because by and large we are, it's a fair generalisation. It is not right to say, 'God, every single one of us is ecstatic to be here', because this is not true. Some of us may be ecstatic, but others will be sad, some guilty, some confused, some desperate, some angry, some afraid. There might well be somebody thinking, 'Why *did* I come this morning?'

You do not want your prayers to make anyone feel pushed out. Instead, your prayers should be realistic about the people present. They should also be realistic about God. Do not make promises that God does not make. It is fine to say that everybody who confesses their sins will be forgiven (1 John 1:9).

It is not fine to say that everyone who becomes a Christian will never have any more problems and will surely win the lottery this week. You do not want your congregation sitting there thinking, 'Hang on, that isn't true!' when they should be concentrating on God. Pray kindly, with encouragement, with love, with forgiveness and without exaggeration, anger or bitterness. Be positive.

Inclusive language

In recent years inclusive language has become an issue. Should you talk about mankind or humankind? Should you talk about God as he, she or it?

Now some older people say that they have been talking about mankind for years and that includes men and women, so what is the problem? But for younger people the language used is a real issue. It is important to include everybody you can and it costs nothing to talk about humankind rather than mankind. St. Paul said in 1 Corinthians 9:20, 'To the Jews I became like a Jew, to win the Jews'. You want to win people, not win arguments. You want people to become Christians, so you should not make it difficult for people to feel part of what you do by your use of language. If singing dreary hymns discourages people from coming, then stop singing them. If using sexist language discourages people from coming, then stop using it. It is not difficult to avoid.

Talking about God is more complicated. Should you call God he, she or it? When you talk about Jesus you have to use 'he', because that is what Jesus was.

He had to be born either male or female because otherwise he would not have been fully human. When you talk about the Holy Spirit, you can use either male or female words. The book of Proverbs (1:20) talks about the 'Wisdom of God' as female, and this 'Wisdom' has traditionally been identified with the Spirit. Using he *or* she for the Spirit is not likely to cause any difficulty, even with a conservative congregation. If you can show something is in the Bible, most Christians will accept it.

The real issue is calling God 'Father'. When you describe God, you go beyond the limits of language. To say God is 'Father' is only an analogy, a picture, because God is more than a father. God is caring like a father; God commands like a father; God disciplines like a father; God brought us into being like a father. But God is not a human being like a father. Nor does our need for a human mother mean that God needs a divine mother to create things. God is only like a father *up to a point*. For instance, God does not embarrass you by complaining about your driving, or by wearing a string vest in public. If your earthly father was not all he should have been, then this analogy could even be harmful in your relationship with God.

God is more than a father, and that is why there are so many ways of describing God in the Bible. The Old Testament says that God is like a father, God is like a mother, God is like a king, God is like a creator, even that God is like a potter. These descriptions are helpful, but only tell part of the story. They can only ever go part of the way. Jesus called God 'Father'. Jesus did not call God 'Mother', but he did not call God 'King' either and the Church does that readily enough. Whatever the words you use to describe God, they do not change the nature of God. God is the one who says, 'I am who I am and I will be who I will be'. Calling God 'King of the universe' does not make God into the king of the universe. If God is King, then God was King before you started saying it.

There is a difference between margarine and butter. You can bring out a new margarine and call it 'This Is Just Like Butter, Honest', but it is still margarine. (And if *you* can't tell the difference, then you should start worrying about your tastebuds!) The substance does not change with the name, *but our ideas do*. If you put margarine on your toast, but tell your children it is butter, then your children will grow up thinking that butter is something that bears only a faint resemblance to the real thing. If you only call God 'Father', then your children will grow up thinking that God is a little grey-haired old man who lives in the sky; which they probably do.

If you want to say that God is more than an old man in the sky (and you *do* want to say that) then you need to come up with other titles. Fortunately, the Bible is full of them, so you have plenty of ways to speak about God. There are lots of good ways of talking about God that do not demand that God is male. Instead of 'Father', you can say 'Parent'. Instead of 'King', you can say 'Ruler'. It is not about political correctness, it is about not limiting

God by your choice of language. Your listeners need not notice it is happening.

The real crunch comes when you decide to redress the imbalance of centuries and call God 'Mother' or 'she'. Your listeners will most definitely notice. Sometimes this is a good thing; they may need shaking out of their complacency and comfort. At other times it can just be destructive. There is a spectrum of views within the churches on this issue. Try to make the effort to think of others as much as you can before making your final stand 'because you can do no other'. Remember, you want to win people, not just arguments.

The Lord's Prayer

Can you have a service without using the Lord's Prayer? Of course you can! However, it is the prayer that Jesus taught us and a lot of people find it helpful. Most churches include it in most of their services. If you are going to use the Lord's Prayer, then a good tip is to have the words written down, because even if you know it back to front, it is easy to make a mistake and cause chaos. I led a service and said, 'Thy will be done, Thy kingdom come, on earth as it is in heaven'. It was very easily done and threw me completely for the rest of the prayers. Nobody complained at the end, but that just shows how people assume that the leader knows how to pray properly!

The congregation needs you to lead loudly and clearly so they can follow. Whether you use the traditional or a modern version depends on you, but check out what the people normally use and stick with that. Remember also that in some places they sing the Lord's Prayer.

Practical praying

So how do you start? Traditionally, with the words, 'Let us pray'. If you want, you can ask the question, 'Shall we pray?' but this risks the response, 'No'.

And how do you finish? Usually with the word, 'Amen', which means either 'so be it' or 'it's a fact'. Be sure to say 'Amen' clearly so people know the prayer has ended.

In between keep it simple and straightforward. Don't rush it. Speaking too quickly can lead to spiritual indigestion. If you go too fast, then people will not have time to join their prayers with yours. Every so often have a short period of silence. For example, 'We give thanks for the good things we have been given, and in the silence we make our own thanksgiving', followed by a short pause (or a long pause if you have a lot for which to give thanks).

Alternatively, you can invite the people to make a response to your prayers. One classic formula is to say, 'Lord, in your mercy', to which they respond, 'Hear our prayer'. When you use such responses, keep them short and simple. If you make them too long, then people will be concentrating on trying to remember the words rather than listening to the prayer.

It may be that you have two sessions of prayer, one near the start of the service and one near the end. It is traditional to put the asking prayers after the others, but you can put things in whatever order you like. As a rule, you ought not to repeat earlier prayers.

Should people sit or kneel? There are many ways of prayer. (See the box.)

Sample prayers

Heavenly Father, we praise you for who you are and give you thanks for what you have done for us:

We praise you for making everything. For . . . (add your own prayers). In the silence we offer our own praises.

We thank you for the good things you have given us. For . . . add your own prayers). In the silence we offer our own thanks.

We thank you for the gift of Jesus.

We are sorry for some of the things we have done, some of the things we have said and some of the things we have thought. For . . . (add your own prayers). In the silence we confess our sins.

Jesus came in to the world to forgive sins. Let us hear the words he spoke so many years ago, yet speaks to each one of us here today, 'Your sins are forgiven'.

We bring before you the needs of the world. For . . . (add your own prayers). We pray for one person we would like to see become a Christian.

We ask all our prayers in the name of Jesus. Amen.

Seven positions in which to pray

☺ The Kneel.
High church. Head up, hands clasped.

☺ Shampoo Crouch.
Low church. Lean forward, head down, hands together.

☺ The Walk.
Pilgrims. Head up, eyes open, sandals on feet.

☺ The Stand.
Charismatic or Eastern Orthodox. Head up, arms up, hands up, looking up. Can be followed by

☺ The Collapse.
Charismatic. Flat out, facing up, movements optional.
Not to be confused with

☺ The Prostrate.
Very high church. Flat out, facing down, no movements at all.

☺ The Upside Down.
Outside church. Hanging from a telegraph pole, foot caught in the wire.
Telephone engineers finding themselves in this situation have reported an amazing new intensity to their prayer life.

Pray without ceasing?

Whatever prayers you use, keep them clear, coherent and concise.

Insalata Tricolore

One avocado   *½lb mozzarella cheese*

One beef tomato   *Black olives*

Olive oil   *Wine vinegar*

Salt and pepper   *Herbs of choice*

This makes a great starter. Slice the tomato thinly and salt. Cut the avocado in half, peel, and then slice flesh thinly. Drain cheese and slice thinly. Arrange slices in three vertical stripes, as in the Italian flag, green, white and red (avocado, cheese, tomato). Arrange the olives at the side, like a flag pole.

Pour olive oil and wine vinegar over to taste. Add pepper and other herbs. Basil or thyme is fine, but garlic is good too. Leave for ten minutes to marinate; serve with Italian bread and butter. Bueno Appetito!

Serves: Two

Calories: An awful lot

Chapter 4

Meat and two veg ———

——— The Bible and the sermon

Chapter 4 is the main course because the word is at the heart of all we do. Both preaching the word and reading the word are important. It *is* possible to have Christian worship without the Bible, but it is a meal with little nourishment.

How many Bible readings should I have?

Traditionally people have put together three readings for a service: one from the Old Testament, one from the Gospels and one from the Epistles. (See the box.)

This is a bit like ordering potatoes and being given baked, boiled and chips. The idea is that the three readings go together and show a common theme. This is not compulsory. If you want to be traditional, then have three readings. If you want to be direct, choose just one. If you are trying to make a point, then keep your reading simple and *make that point*. Don't weaken the message by diffusing the issue.

Whatever readings you use, try to keep them short. Just a few verses are enough. Most people start listening, but after the first couple of verses they drift off. To make your impact, don't read for too long. Three lengthy readings can lose people completely. If you

> ## What is an epistle?
>
> An epistle is just a fancy word for a letter. In the early church people sent each other letters, and some of them have found their way into our Bible, because they contain such important truths.
>
> The New Testament also contains The Acts of the Apostles and Revelation, which are not really letters at all. Acts is the history of the early Church and Revelation is a vision of things to come. However these two books are usually lumped together with the 'real' Epistles.
>
> So you could say that the Epistle comes from anywhere in the New Testament that is not a Gospel and you would be right.

need to read a lot of verses to get the sense of the whole story, give a summary at the beginning or the end.

Can I start in the middle of a chapter?

You can start exactly where you like, in the middle of a chapter or even in the middle of a verse. There is no right or wrong place to start. The individual

Chapter and verse

An English Cardinal called Stephen Langton (1155-1228) did the chapter divisions as part of his commentaries on the Bible. He seems to have been an important man of his time, as his name appears as first witness on the Magna Carta.

A Parisian printer named Robert Stephanus (1503-1559) did the first verse divisions in his Greek New Testament of 1551. An unknown Rabbi had worked on the Old Testament about twenty years previously.

books in the New Testament were finished by AD 200. For the next couple of centuries there were disputes as to which books were genuine. The final decision on what should actually *be* in the Bible was not made until AD 376. Chapters did not appear until 800 years later; verses another 300 years after that.

This means that the Bible existed as books, but without chapter and verse, for 1500 years, and in the case of the Old Testament, far longer. Furthermore, the people who divided up the Bible did not always necessarily get it right. (See the box.)

Which version shall I use?

There are literally thousands of different translations of the Bible. Just about every language under the sun now has a Bible, and even as you are reading this,

there are people working away translating it into new dialects. They do not start with an English version, but with the earliest available writings.

Generally, the Old Testament was written in Hebrew and the New Testament was written in Greek. For a thousand years the Western Church used the Bible in Latin. This meant that only the priests could understand what the Bible was about. English translations did not start to appear in full until the Wycliffe version in 1382.

Wycliffe translated from the Latin; William Tyndale translated directly from the Greek and produced an English New Testament in 1525. Miles Coverdale produced the first complete English printed Bible in 1535. All three translators suffered an unenviable fate.

Bad to verse

Paul's famous passage on love in 1 Corinthians starts in chapter 13 with 'If I speak in the voice . . . '. Most scholars think that the chapters and verses are wrong, and that the passage really starts at the end of Chapter 12, with 'And now I will show you the most excellent way: If I speak in the voice . . . '.

For this reason you will sometimes see a Bible reference that looks like this: 1 Cor 12:31b. This means First Letter to the Corinthians, chapter 12, second half of verse 31. Because Stephen Langton and Robert Stephanus were not always correct, you can break a verse and still be right.

The tide was turning and in 1611, the Authorised or King James Version appeared. It was put together by 47 academics, and represented the finest scholarship of the day. It was a literary masterpiece and had a tremendous impact on the English-speaking world. So many words, so many turns of phrase, so many quotations came from its pages. This translation was made from the original languages, but still owes some of its phrasing to the hard work of Wycliffe, Tyndale and Coverdale.

The problem is that languages develop and change, and now the words used in the King James Bible are well out of date.

Secondly, the Bible is not meant to be a literary masterpiece. You are not supposed to be impressed by the majesty of the Bible, but you are supposed to be impressed by the majesty of God, as found in the Bible. Just as we do not worship statues or graven images, so we do not worship a book. The Word of God is not the Bible, but Jesus himself. It is a sin (called Bibliolatry) to make an idol out of the Bible, and it is a sin to make an idol out of the magnificent language of the King James version.

In the original Greek, Mark's Gospel is not a great work of art, but a stumbling, jerky, quickly told story. Mark wants to let you know all about the Good News of Jesus Christ as quickly and simply as he can, so he leaves out the finer parts of grammar and style. And he begins lots of sentences with 'and'.

Because of the King James version, English-speaking people assume that

Pastor Ludd taught his congregation that if the King James Bible was good enough for St Paul, it was good enough for them.

© Gospel Films, Inc. – www.reverendfun.com

the Bible is 'highbrow' and that modern translations are not as good. In fact much of the Bible is 'lowbrow' and written by the common people, for the common people, in the language of the marketplace, complete with slang, bad grammar and lack of style. The whole point is that the Bible was written for everybody, so that they could understand and know the love of God and the stories of God's people.

That is why the Bible did not appear in English for so many hundreds of years. The Church wanted to keep the knowledge and power in its own hands. That is why the Bible was banned in Russia during the communist years. It was far too dangerous a book. That is why Bible translators are such persecuted people. (See the box.)

If you want your congregation to be impressed by great literature, read them Shakespeare, or organise a poetry recital. If you want your congregation to understand God's story, then choose the simplest and most straightforward translation of the Bible you can find.

Seven Bible translators

☺ St Jerome (345-420?)
Translated the Bible into Latin.
In hiding for two years.

☺ John Wycliffe (c. 1330-1384)
Translated the Bible into
English. Accused of heresy 1377.
His followers had a brawl with
the Bishop. Accused again in
1378, convicted 1382. In 1428
his body was dug up and burned.

☺ Christiern Pedersen (1480-1554)
Translated the Bible into Danish.
In exile for seven years.

☺ Martin Luther (1483-1546)
Translated the Bible into
German. Banned and
excommunicated.

☺ Miles Coverdale (1488?-1569)
Translated the Bible into
English. Was in exile eight years,
imprisoned for two years, a
further eight years in exile.

☺ William Tyndale (1492?-1536)
Translated the Bible into
English. Strangled and burnt at
the stake.

☺ John Williams (1796-1839)
Translated the New Testament
into Raratongan. Landed as a
missionary at Erromanga and
was struck on the head and
killed.

And countless others were persecuted,
right through to the present day,
which just goes to show how life-
changing a book the Bible is, when
people get to understand it in their
own language. If it were not so power-
ful, they wouldn't bother banning it
and persecuting those who translate it.

Modern translations

The *Revised Version* of the New Testament appeared in 1881 and of the Old
Testament in 1885. In some places, the
King James Bible was just plain wrong
because it depended on the scholarship
of the seventeenth century. New, earlier
Greek manuscripts had been discovered in the intervening years and had
to be taken into account. The *Revised
Version* corrected the errors, but kept
the style of language.

This century (1946-1952), in Amer-
ica, saw the production of the *Revised
Standard Version* (RSV). The RSV
hoped to be both accurate and more
readable. Significantly, the language
was updated. The *New Revised Standard Version* (NRSV) appeared in 1989
with the aim of eliminating all the old-
fashioned words and removing sexist
language wherever possible.

After the Second World War, the
New English Bible (NEB) was con-
ceived and finally produced in 1970.
The idea was to step away from the old
versions and to make a completely new
Bible, from the original languages. The
English would be modern in every

You want modern? You got it!

© Gospel Films, Inc. – www.reverendfun.com

40

way: modern words and modern grammar. Unfortunately, the English language has changed so quickly that even the NEB now seems old-fashioned. This is why the *Revised English Bible* (REB) came along in 1989. It was designed to have 'dignity, fluency, and power . . . with direct expression and elegance of style' and was a direct successor to the NEB. The REB is an excellent Bible for public use.

The *Jerusalem Bible* (JB) was originally a French translation, appearing in 1956. It was so good, and had such excellent footnotes and reference material with it, that an English version was started straight away, appearing in 1966. The style of the different books in the Bible comes through clearly. Poetry is printed as verse and prose as prose. This contrasts with the *King James Bible* which has one style throughout.

The *New International Version* (NIV) was an American project, appearing in 1973. Its aim was to be accurate and readable. Many British churches have standardised on the NIV for the pulpit and pews. The NIV is an excellent Bible for public use.

The *Good News Bible* (GNB) uses standard, everyday, ordinary English. It first appeared in 1966 and was designed to make the Bible understandable to everybody. It modernised the language, broke the text up into paragraphs and made every effort to use words that were natural, clear and simple, so that the original meaning might come through. This Bible also comes with line drawings. The GNB is an excellent Bible for public use.

Can I make my own translation?

Yes. You can, if you know what you are doing and go back to the original Hebrew and Greek.

However, it is a grave mistake to translate from old English to modern English. Here is an example:

In the KJB, Psalm 135:4 reads, 'For the Lord hath chosen Jacob unto himself, and Israel for his peculiar treasure.' Asked to translate this into modern English, we might create, 'For the Lord has chosen Jacob for himself, and Israel for his bizarre treasure'. But we would be wrong. The word 'peculiar' in the seventeenth century meant something different from what it means now.

The REB has, 'For the Lord has chosen Jacob to be his own, Israel as his treasured possession.' The REB biblical scholars were paid a fortune (well, maybe not quite a fortune) to do all the research in the original languages to make the best translation. You can rest assured they did a good job. You don't need to second-guess them.

Avoid making your own translation unless you really know what you are doing.

Paraphrases

To paraphrase is to say the same thing in different words. Paraphrases of the Bible give the Bible message in other words.

The Bible is a complicated collection of books. Sometimes people have tried to turn it into a novel, or a play or some other literary form. They try to keep the sense of what is written, but move away from a direct, literal translation. The problem is that the further you move away from the text, the more an individual's interpretation creeps in. Paraphrases of the Bible include JB Phillips, *The Living Bible*, *The Message*, Alan Dale's *New World* and *Winding Quest*, and the *Dramatised Bible*.

A paraphrase is a bit like powdered potato. It has the form of the original, but is not quite the real thing. If you do use one, which you can, explain what you are doing. It is fine to serve real potato. It *is* fine to serve powdered potato. It is not fine to serve powdered potato and tell people it is real!

Most Bibles are available in large print versions . . .

© Gospel Films, Inc. – www.reverendfun.com

Why can't they all agree and produce one Bible?

Because it is not that easy. Let's look at a simple example and see how hard modern-day Bible translators have to work. Luke 20:24a has the simple sentence of Jesus, 'Show me a denarius' in the NIV. How did we get to those words?

We have to go back to the earliest Greek manuscripts. Nearly all of them say '*deixate moi denarion*'. Literally that means 'show to me denarius'. However, there is a fifth century manuscript in the Cambridge University Library which has the words '*deixate moi to nomisma*' instead, which means 'Show to me the coin'. We'll go with the majority texts and stick with 'denarius'. Then we change our literal translation 'Show to me denarius' into the more pleasing 'Show me a denarius'. The *Jerusalem Bible* agrees with the NIV. The RSV says, 'Show me a coin' but the NRSV goes back to 'Show me a denarius'.

That's fine for scholars of the ancient world who know that a denarius was a coin with Caesar's head on it, which was worth about a day's wages. But what about ordinary people who do not know that? What then?

We can try to carry through the meaning of 'denarius' by using today's money. The *King James Bible* did just that for the seventeenth century reader when it said, 'Shew me a penny'. That still works for this passage, but in Matthew 20:2 a landowner pays his workers a denarius a day, which the KJB translates as a penny a day. That doesn't make much sense in these inflationary times.

The GNB says 'Show me a silver coin'. (Maybe if Hollywood did the translation they would come up with 'Show me the money!') The NEB and the REB say, 'Show me a silver piece'. The *Living Bible* says, 'Show me a coin'. These have the advantage of being timeless and not worrying about inflation, and bringing through the meaning. They have the disadvantage that nearly every original manuscript says 'denarius', not 'coin'.

For personal study, it is best to be as close to the original as possible, so 'denarius' would be preferred. For reading out loud, especially to people who are not experts, 'silver coin' or 'silver piece' make easier hearing and are the preferred translations. 'Penny', from the KJB, scrapes by in this passage, but just sounds odd elsewhere and should be avoided.

Now that particular sentence is not controversial, and yet we have already seen that there are several different ways of translating it. Just imagine the problems that there are when:

(a) The ancient texts disagree. Occasionally there are significant differences between ancient manuscripts. Bible translators have to choose which they think is the original. Sometimes bits are missing altogether like Mark 16:9-20, which many people think is a later addition. In these circumstances it is a matter of at least a PhD to be able to make a considered judgement.

(b) The ancient texts do not make sense. This is particularly a problem in Hebrew, where there are no vowels and you have to try to guess what they would have been. This can lead to inventiveness. For some passages, with the best will in the world, and the best scholarship, there is no single, clear, translation. (See the box.)

(c) The ancient texts have no punctuation marks. Is it a question, a statement or a quotation? 1 Corinthians 8:1b says, 'We know that we all have knowledge'. But is St Paul quoting a letter that the Corinthians have written to him? The REB translates it as 'Of course "we all have knowledge" as you say'. Because there is no punctuation we cannot tell.

This also applies to instructions. The verb endings are the same in some cases. The same words can mean 'Pray continually' or 'Let us pray continually'.

(d) The subject is controversial. Philippians 1:1 talks about the *'episkopoi'* and *'diakonoi'*. The KJB calls these 'bishops and deacons', as does the RSV and NRSV. The *Jerusalem Bible* talks about 'presiding elders and deacons'. The NIV says 'overseers and deacons' and the GNB says 'church leaders and helpers'.

What this goes to prove is that, while most people are happy with the idea of deacons, the question of bishops is more problematic. Did the early Church have bishops as we know them, or not? Nobody knows the answer to this question, but what you believe does have an influence on how you will translate the Bible. There seems to be about an equal amount of evidence on both sides and there was a diversity

Hard words, hard to understand

Let's look at the Book of Isaiah, and a lament about the evil that people do. Chapter 5:17 is very difficult to translate. Here are some attempts.

KJV – Then shall the lambs feed after their manner, and the waste places of the fat ones shall strangers eat.

GNB – In the ruins of the cities lambs will eat grass and young goats will find pasture.

NIV – Then sheep will graze as in their own pasture; lambs will feed among the ruins of the rich.

JB – Lambs will graze as at pasture, fatlings and kids browse in the ruins.

NRSV – Then the lambs shall graze as in their pasture, fatlings and kids shall feed among the ruins.

REB – Lambs will feed where fat bullocks once pastured, young goats will graze broad acres where cattle grew fat.

Literal translation of Septuagint (Greek OT) – 'And they that were spoiled shall be fed as bulls, and lambs shall feed on the waste places of them that are taken away.'

Literal translation of the Hebrew: very difficult to make out.

Different translations

So there are in existence several different translations of the Bible into English, and the number will continue to grow. It may be appropriate to use one translation of the Bible for personal study and another for reading out loud in public. Remember, you want all the people hearing you to understand your message as clearly as possible, therefore the simpler the translation and the easier it reads, the better.

These days, many churches have Bibles in the seats for the congregation to follow. Even if you are not that keen on the translation used, it makes sense to follow it. Don't start off with: 'Now I know you have the *Good News Bible* out there, but this says what I want it to say in the NIV . . . '

Bibliomancy

It is *not* a good idea to open the Bible at random and put your finger on a verse with your eyes closed. This is called 'Bibliomancy'. Often the book will fall open at the same page, giving the same message over and over again.

Then there is the well-known curse which comes from finding Matthew 27:5 'And Judas . . . went away and hanged himself', followed by Luke 10:37: 'Go and do thou likewise.'

This is *not* a message from God. You should take responsibility for the passage chosen and this is not the way to do it.

of practice in the early Church. Some Bibles have a translation of 'bishops', other Bibles say 'overseers'. Maybe the word chosen says more about the translators than about the original manuscripts . . .

Which reading should I choose?

A lot of the time you will not have to worry about this. If somebody else is giving a talk or a sermon, then they probably have chosen a reading already.

If you still have to choose, then a good way is to use a *lectionary*. For every Sunday in the year there are set readings, so all you have to do is find the set reading for the day. Sometimes these readings suggest themselves, especially at seasons of the year such as Christmas and Easter.

If even the lectionary does not help, or you cannot find one, how do you decide which reading to use?

Which are the best bits of the Bible?

In a way, this is the wrong question to ask, because every part of the Bible is there for a reason. But not every Bible passage is equally helpful for public worship.

One approach is to use a *concordance* or a Bible software program. Both allow you to search for particular words or phrases, one manually, the other electronically. If you cannot afford either of those, and they can be expensive, try a local library or college. They should have an internet connection and you can search on-line. When you want a passage which mentions 'casting the first stone', hopefully you will be pointed to John 8:7.

Books of the Bible:

Old Testament
Genesis, Exodus, Leviticus, Numbers, Deuteronomy.
Joshua, Judges, Ruth.
1 Samuel, 2 Samuel, 1 Kings, 2 Kings, 1 Chronicles, 2 Chronicles.
Ezra, Nehemiah.
Esther, Job, Psalms, Proverbs, Ecclesiastes, Song of Solomon.
Isaiah, Jeremiah, Lamentations, Ezekiel.
Daniel, Hosea, Joel, Amos, Obadiah, Jonah, Micah, Nahum, Habakkuk, Zephaniah, Haggai, Zechariah, Malachi.

New Testament
Matthew, Mark, Luke, John.
Acts of the Apostles.
Romans, 1 Corinthians, 2 Corinthians, Galatians, Ephesians, Philippians, Colossians, 1 Thessalonians, 2 Thessalonians, 1 Timothy, 2 Timothy, Titus, Philemon.
Hebrews, James, 1 Peter, 2 Peter.
1 John, 2 John, 3 John, Jude, Revelation.

Another approach is to use a study Bible. A study Bible includes an introduction to each book, which gives you a little information about its background and the stories included. Study Bibles are available in most translations.

Some people say that the Bible is so special that every verse is important. This is true, but it is also true that some verses are more helpful than others. When you are leading worship you want to use the passages that are the most 'suitable', that is to say, those passages that are clear, understandable and relevant. If the meaning of a passage is not clear, then it might be good to study it in a small group, but it is not very helpful in public worship. If a passage cannot be understood then it is of little benefit. If a passage talks about a subject that does not relate to today (for example Leviticus 13:47ff on 'mildew') it will not help or instruct the listeners.

That does not mean your readings cannot be challenging. Much of the Bible does challenge our complacency. Mark Twain said that the things in the Bible he could not understand didn't worry him half as much as the things in the Bible he *could* understand.

Apocryphal books

Tobit

Judith

Esther (Greek) or Additions to Esther

Wisdom of Solomon

Wisdom of Ben Sirach or
    Ecclesiasticus

Baruch

Letter of Jeremiah

Prayer of Azariah

Susanna

Bel and the Dragon

1 Maccabees, 2 Maccabees,
    3 Maccabees and 4 Maccabees

1 Esdras, 2 Esdras

Prayer of Manasseh

Psalm 151

My Bible has other books in it. Does this matter?

These other books are called the *Apocrypha*, which means 'hidden writings'. They are extra books that were written in the troubled times between the Old and New Testaments. Some are additions to Old Testament books, like Daniel or the Book of Psalms. Others are works in their own right.

In some Bibles these extra books are fitted between the Old and New Testaments. In others they appear among the Old Testament books. It would not usually be appropriate to use apocryphal writings in public worship in a protestant church.

I don't know a lot about the Bible. Does this matter?

Not at all. The Bible is meant to be read. It does not matter if you have never heard about Marcan priority or the Synoptic problem. You do not have to be a food scientist to be able to cook well. In fact, food science and cooking are two different and separate disciplines. So are Bible scholarship and worship. You do not have to be a Bible scholar to lead worship.

When you are making gravy, a food scientist will tell you that after you heat food starches to a certain point they will change and thicken into dextrins.

Knowing that theory will not necessarily stop you having lumpy gravy. A biblical scholar can tell you the latest theories on the works of St Paul. Knowing the theory will not necessarily give you good worship.

Let me tell you more about the Synoptic Problem . . .

© Gospel Films, Inc. – www.reverendfun.com

Important book

The Bible is the most important book in the world. Read it to your people.

Should I preach a sermon?

That is a good question. Leading worship is one thing. Preaching is different altogether.

Preaching is taking the word in the Bible and making it the word for today. Preaching is interpreting the word and explaining it. Preaching is the truth through personality. The Word of God still has an impact today. A sermon does not have to be dreary, it does not have to be irrelevant, it does not have to have three points and it does not

have to be twenty minutes long. Like the rest of worship, a sermon should be simple but profound. It should be possible to sum up the aim of a sermon in one sentence. If that cannot be done, then the sermon is not direct enough.

The sermon should be simple in that it uses ordinary words, ideas and illustrations. The sermon should be profound in that it looks at the questions people are really asking, which are about relationships, money, crime and death, just like the Gospels. The secret is to use the language of the marketplace to study the essentials of theology, not the other way round.

Maybe you feel that God has called you to lead worship. Maybe you think that God has called you to preach. This is not the book to help you decide whether you should become a preacher. That book is *The Joy of Preaching* by Phillips Brooks, the man who wrote the carol *O Little Town of Bethlehem*. (See chapter 12 for details.) It is a great book and well worth the read anyway. You will find it very helpful.

The Bible readings are like the vegetables in a meal – nourishing in their own right, providing sustenance and vitality. The sermon is like the meat, something that can be the centre of the entire meal, or something that can be tough as old boots! With vegetables you cannot go too far wrong, as long as you don't overcook them. With the Bible readings you cannot go too far wrong, because they stand by themselves.

The meat is more difficult. If you do not cook the meat properly, you can end up poisoning your guests. In the same way, a bad sermon can be terribly destructive and poisonous to its hearers. One of the biggest obstacles to faith can be the unhelpful words of insensitive Christians.

If preaching is not for you, then do not feel tempted just to 'say a few words'. Don't get carried away into making your own explanations of the way things are. If you are going to preach, then do it properly and train and study to do it the best you can. If you do feel called to preach, then that is excellent, and you should have a word with your church leaders about it. They will be able to point you in the right direction.

If you do not feel called to preach, but do feel called to lead worship, then that is excellent too, because leading worship is an important gift in itself. Give it a try!

Gravy

Meat or vegetable juices
Tablespoon of flour

Pour the juices from the meat into a pan. Heat until nearly boiling. Very gradually add the sifted flour, stirring all the while. Failure to stir will lead to lumpy gravy. Bring to the boil and simmer for two minutes. Serve hot.

Chapter 5
Pudding

The music

I have compared music to the pudding, but not because it has to be last on the menu. As we have seen, order does not matter. But often, when you finish a meal, it is the pudding you remember. In the same way, when you leave worship, it is the songs that most readily come to mind. The prayers, the talk, the silences may all have been excellent, but it is the taste of the music that remains.

There are three things to consider when choosing a song: the tune, the tune and the tune. No matter how good the words are, if the tune is unsingable, then don't bother. If the words are great, then read them as a poem. Don't try and sing them. If you have a perfect piece of fruit you would serve it fresh. You would not spoil it by stewing it. If you have a great piece of poetry, you should read it as it is. You should not spoil it by singing it to the tune of the *Funeral March*.

Ideally, the morning after worship, people should be humming the tune of your last song, and hopefully remembering the words. There is a story told that Paul McCartney knew that The Beatles had *really* made it when he heard the milkman whistling one of his tunes. If the melody is dreary, then it will not be remembered with any fondness. If your pudding is stodgy, people will forget all the good things that came before.

It *is* possible to change the tune of many songs by picking a different melody in the same metre. Songs have different numbers of lines, and different rhythms within those lines, but there are many common forms. Thus, the traditional Easter hymn *There is a green hill far away* can be sung to the tunes of *Amazing grace, The Lord's my Shepherd, On Ilkley Moor bah'tat* or even *The House of the Rising Sun* (to which it goes very well). (See the box on 'Metre' for how to change the tune of a song.)

When you have picked your tunes, the other thing you have to make sure is that your musicians can play them. If you are very fortunate, you will have the kind of people who can play anything you give them on any instrument, like the late Roy Castle, who could even play the teapot. But what if your musicians are not virtuosos? The simple alternative is to let them choose the music and the tunes. After all, they know what they can play, and they know what the local people like. It is good to have lots of people involved in worship and to trust others to make their contribution. However, if they don't want to make the selection, then what do you do? How easy should you make the tunes? And how can you tell if a tune is difficult, particularly if you are unable to read music? (See the box.)

How to read the metre

Every poem has a metre; that is, a length and a rhythm. To stop poets going 'dum diddi dum dum' when they are describing the rhythm, there is a special code. Each syllable is called a foot. (Now we've got feet and metres. Confusing, isn't it?). Let's look at a well-known hymn and count the feet.

There is a green hill far a-way (8)
with-out a ci-ty wall (6)
where the dear Lord was
    cru-ci-fied. (8)
He died to save us all (6)

So the first line has 8 feet, the second 6 feet, the third 8 feet and the fourth 6 feet. Thus the metre of this hymn is 86.86. This is so often used that it is called Common Metre, or CM for short. There are also Short Metre (SM) which is 66.86 and Long Metre (LM) which is 88.88. A six line hymn will have a six digit metre. Thus *Once in Royal David's City* is 87.87.77.

You will find the metre in music copies of your songbook, at the top left, next to the name of the tune. Many choruses won't have such a structured rhythm, so they may not have a metre.

When you have found the metre of your song, and want to change the tune, look in the back of your music copy at the Metrical Index. This groups together tunes which fit the same metre. Choose a more appropriate tune from the ones listed. If there are no alternatives, or none suitable, then you'll have to stick with what you've got.

But what happens if you choose the tunes and the organist can only play them slowly? How can you speed things up without dosing the tea with Turbo-Lax?

You could ask nicely. Many organists play slowly because they think the congregation can only sing slowly. I play the guitar, and there are times when I have come racing in with an introduction at one pace, only for the people to sing at half-speed. It could even be that your organist agrees with you and wants things to be faster. If you have been asked to lead worship for a one-off event, then you will just have to live with what you have. Musicians can be notoriously temperamental. Some people say the difference between an organist and a terrorist is that you can negotiate with a terrorist, but I couldn't possibly comment.

In the long term, for the health of the church, no one person can have a veto on the music. Outsiders are not going to stay if the music is awful. Evangelism is easy. If your worship is great, then you will tell people about it naturally and invite them along. If your worship sometimes makes you cringe, so that you dare not invite any of your friends, then it is time to change the worship. There is no point evangelising people into coming to a kind of worship to which they will not return. A restaurant with bad food will close, no matter how good the advertising. A church with dire music will go the same way. If that means you have to change the musicians, *then so be it*. It is one thing if your musicians are not experts yet do their best. God loves

How hard is the music?

Music is usually written on a five line scale. For traditional hymns there will be an upper scale, the treble clef, and a lower scale, the bass clef.

The treble clef looks something like this. The numbers on the right are the time signature. 3/4 time is waltz time. We needn't worry about that. The two slightly squashed 'b's are the key signature. These are flats, or lowered notes. If a note is to be raised, then we would see a '#' or sharp in the key signature.

No sharps or flats at all means play only the white keys on a piano. This is the easiest key, C Major. One sharp or flat means play one black key. Two sharps or flats mean playing two black keys. This is harder. The more sharps or flats, the harder it is. More than five sharps means giving up on the black keys and going back to the white keys again. This can only be performed by concert pianists working overtime.

The notes are the black dots on the lines. The more there are to the inch, the more difficult it is to play. Lots of words in Italian is also a bad sign.

humility in worship. It is another thing altogether when they are deliberately difficult and refuse to play what you have chosen.

What can you do then? One thing you could try is to announce, 'We shall now sing the Isaac Watts hymn *Come, we that love the Lord*, commencing at verse 3, which I shall now read:

Let those refuse to sing
that never knew our God;
but children of the heavenly King
may speak their joys abroad.'

In the final analysis, it is better to pay somebody to play than to have a volunteer who does not have the best interests of the whole church at heart.

Which songs to choose?

Fine, so you won't choose anything too stodgy, you will make sure that the tunes are singable, you will make sure your musicians can play them, but what songs should you choose and how many of them? The number of songs is entirely up to you. At a Quaker service there would probably be no music. At the 'happy-clappy' charismatics you could have a dozen choruses before they've even started. You know what your people like. If you don't, then for goodness sake ask them! Bear in mind, however, that if you have been asked to lead worship for the runners at the end of the city marathon, then fewer will be better than more.

When you lead worship, you can *choose any songs you want*. They can be traditional, modern, played on organ, guitar, piano, or trumpet; they can be slow or be fast, whatever you like. You do *not* have to choose songs that fit your theme. When cooking a meal, you would not choose a pudding to go with beef, lamb or pork unless you were really fussy. You would pick a pudding that was worthwhile in its own right. When preparing worship, you do not have to pick songs that go with your prayers and readings, unless you want to be fussy. People remember the tunes. They hardly ever consciously take in the words. They will sing virtually any words that are put in front of them, without noticing. They will hymn the merits of Ebenezers, seraphs, cherubim, and crystal seas, without having any idea what they are or where they come from. (See the box for an explanation of unusual hymn words.)

Seven unusual words found in hymns

☺ Cherubim Animal-like angels
Genesis 3:24

☺ Crystal sea A sea of glass in front of the throne of God.
Revelations 4:6

☺ Ebenezer Stone of help
1 Samuel 7:12

☺ Oblation An offering
Isaiah 1:13

☺ Paraclete Comforter
John 14:16

☺ Seraph Six-winged angel
Isaiah 6:2

☺ Veil A barrier between us and God.
2 Corinthians 3:13-16

So, if you choose songs that fit your theme but are difficult to sing, then there are very few people who will appreciate your efforts. But if you choose songs which the people can sing out, expressing their faith in music, they will enjoy the worship. Most songs do go with most themes. And if your theme is contradicted by lots of hymns, then maybe it is time to change your theme. Obviously there are seasonal variations for Christmas, Easter and Harvest, but apart from those you should be free to choose.

It is difficult to think of a service where *Amazing grace* would not be appropriate. It can be sung at any season of the year, during baptisms, weddings, funerals, ordinations, children's parties and football matches. It can be played on keyboard, bagpipes, guitar (3 chord, 12 bar blues) and recorder. It can be sung slowly or quickly, but never loses its form. There are many other songs just as useful. (See the box.)

Seven songs for any occasion

☺ All things bright and beautiful

☺ At the name of Jesus

☺ Bind us together

☺ Hallelujah, sing to Jesus

☺ Praise my soul the King of Heaven

☺ Shine, Jesus, shine

☺ When I survey the wondrous cross

If you are doing a one-off service, then it is perfectly acceptable to choose your own favourites. But if you are leading worship 52 weeks a year, people may get fed up with *Bringing in the sheaves* every time. When you do introduce new material, it is only fair to introduce it gradually so that folk can get used to it. Once again, the stronger the tune, the easier it is to learn. If the tune is already well known, then you can use the song as if it were an old standard. The Methodist hymn writer, Charles Wesley, set many of the hymns he wrote to folk songs of the day, which helped the people (a lot of whom could not read) to remember his hymns. Interestingly, football crowds today have returned the compliment and set some of their songs to hymn tunes. (See the box.)

Seven hymns that football crowds sing (sometimes with different words)

- ☺ Abide with me
- ☺ God save the Queen
- ☺ Lord of the dance
- ☺ Mary's boy child
- ☺ Mine eyes have seen the glory of the coming of the Lord
- ☺ O come, all ye faithful
- ☺ O when the saints go marching in

Which songbook should you use? For most people, this choice will have already been made for them. It is no use picking songs from the latest edition when the congregation uses *Ancient & More Ancient – A Hymnbook for Yesterday's Church*. Do the best with what you have. A *real* cook can pro-

duce something good even with limited ingredients. If you do take songs from other books, then remember copyright laws, which are always more strict than people imagine. There is a way round this. Check the list of useful addresses in Chapter 12 for copyright licensing.

On a practical note, not everybody can read, although we often assume that they can. If you need five different books and a handful of pieces of paper to follow your worship, then you are making it difficult for people. An overhead projector can help, and if you have a colour or a symbol to go with each song (a star for *Shine, Jesus, shine*) then the non-literate will know which one it is and be able to join in more easily.

Don't be worried about outsiders either. They would prefer to sing words they *don't* understand to a tune they *do*, rather than the other way round. There is a sense in which however open we think the words are that we use in songs, people from outside will not understand. As in Matthew 13:13 ' . . . hearing they hear not, neither do they understand'. So if what we do is hard to understand anyway, we may as well do it to a good tune as not.

If you are in any doubt as to the lack of significance of words in singing, then consider this. At one end of the spectrum there are Cathedral choirs singing in Latin. At the other end, one of the greatest songs in pop history (in my opinion) starts off 'Alamba-maloombam alambamboom'. What does that mean? And yet it is still a great song!

If words *were* that important, then operas would be in English. And if words were important then they would not have let Frank Sinatra 'doobie-doo' when he forgot them. And if words were so important, Shakespeare would be at the top of the charts, not pop music. There are very few people in the country who wish this were the case (the same ones who are hoping that wind-up gramophones will return and that computers will be banned in favour of typewriters). (See the box.)

On the other hand, we do not just sing 'la' to the hymns and choruses we have each Sunday. Words *can* matter in the sense that people take them in *subconsciously*. People learn about God from hymns they sing week in and week out.

When people are in nursing homes, perhaps suffering from Alzheimer's disease, sometimes the last things they can remember are the Lord's Prayer, and their favourite hymns. Naturally, these are the ones with the good tunes.

If words were important . . .

If words were important, then half the songs we sing would have to go. Apart from the Ebenezers and crystal seas, there are:

- The sentimental. *Gentle Jesus, meek and mild.* If he'd been that meek and mild they wouldn't have crucified him.

- The theologically over-technical. *Blessed City, Heavenly Salem.* Verse 5: 'Consubstantial, co-eternal, while unending ages run.' It's good to stretch your people, but not this much.

- The embarrassingly imperialistic. *I vow to thee my country.* All verses.

- The embarrassingly militaristic. *Onward Christian soldiers.* All verses.

- The downright embarrassing. *Lord, you put a tongue in my mouth.* This can only be sung by the very pure, when there are no visitors.

- The confusing. *Mine eyes have seen the glory of the coming of the Lord.* Verse 3: 'In the beauty of the lilies Christ was born across the sea'. This is a reference to Matthew 6:28, but makes it sound as if Jesus was born in a florist's.

- The overstatements. *We plough the fields and scatter.* We don't any more. A farmer does it for us.

- The heretical. *O loving Lord, who art for ever seeking.* Verse 3: 'Through faithful service cometh full salvation.' This is just not true! Through Jesus Christ cometh full salvation. We cannot earn salvation by good works. Bible Reference: the entire New Testament.

If words *did* matter, we wouldn't sing these songs, would we? Words should be simple but profound.

What this means is that people will remember the words of hymns that they sang as children, week by week. They won't remember words you sing one time only.

The classic songs of the Christian Church need to have good words. Hymns and choruses that you are not going to be singing every week don't have to be restricted by such stringent limitations. It is better that people enjoy their worship singing simple yet profound hymns rather than theologically sophisticated dirges.

Choose the hymns and choruses that you want. In all cases, they still have to be sung to good tunes.

Other singing

You've chosen your songs, and the people can sing them. You've picked the right number of songs for your people, and have decided whereabouts in the menu you're going to serve them. Then you remember the choir. They like to sing an *anthem*. (See the box.)

There are three things that cause real trouble in churches. Outsiders might think it would be theological disputes that divide people, but in reality it is the flowers, the youth club and *the choir*. Some choirs think that they can sing, even when they can't. It's a bit like preparing a meal and then discovering that Aunty Ethel has brought along her home-made trifle. Not only do you have to eat it (however inedible), but you also have to thank Aunty Ethel profusely; otherwise she gets upset.

How to tell the difference between a song and an anthem

A song might have the words:
'The cow is in the corn'.

An anthem would have the words:
'The cow is in the corn.

The corn, the corn, the golden corn.

The cow is in the corn. The cow is, the cow is, the cow is, the cow is, the cow is, in that golden corn.

Where's that cow? It's in the corn.

Is it in the corn? Yes, the cow is in the corn, the corn, the corn, the golden corn.

Are you sure it's in the corn?

The cow is in the corn. The cow is in the corn.'

Also, in most songs people all sing together. This is called 'unison'. In an anthem different people will sing different tunes. This is called 'harmony' (theoretically). Some of the finest religious works ever written are anthems, such as Handel's *Messiah*. Unfortunately there is a lot of dated material in the repertoire of many choirs. For balance, you could ask the choir to sing anthems written since 1980 every other week. This would encourage them to use new material, without alienating them by rejecting the past out of hand.

Basically, you're on your own here. The easiest thing would be to ask the choir not to sing an anthem this week, but this is not always popular with them. Collaboration with the choir leader is another option, but remember that in the end collaborators get shot. If you are lucky, the choir will sing modern pieces that enthuse the congregation and everybody around. If you are unlucky, they won't. If you have got a good choir, be grateful. They are hard to find.

The same goes for soloists. Try to push them kicking and screaming forward into the nineteenth century. Variations on *Come into the garden, Maude* and other 'singalonga-Queen-Victoria' are not the only options. All sorts of musical styles can be very effective, including Country and Western, Soul, even Rap. Why not expand your congregation's musical horizons? You'd be surprised how many people can play an instrument these days, although not necessarily the keyboard.

Anybody can worship. Anybody can lead worship. Ask your people, especially your young people what they can play. Failing that, stand well back. Worship, like the faith itself, is all about pointing away from the human towards the divine. The danger with soloists is that they do the opposite. If your soloists will not sing when you want them to, refer back to *Let those refuse to sing* on page 51.

Some churches these days have music groups. If you have one, try to get them to cover a broad range of material. Give them the responsibility and the power to choose all the music and watch them grow. *Involvement* is much more than *participation*. Involvement in worship means that they choose. Participation in worship means that they play your choices. *Real* involvement is the ideal. If the music group is made up of young people, then be especially forgiving and encourage them as much as possible.

However, even with modern material and a contemporary outlook, a music group can get in the same rut as the traditional choir. Today's innovation can be tomorrow's inelasticity. Try to keep the group fresh.

Other music

It's very trendy to have music playing so that people can meditate as they listen. Often this is accompanied by worthy slides of pretty flowers and interesting landscapes. It is bad enough having to watch somebody's holiday slides in their home without getting them at church as well, but if you really must, then go ahead.

Alternatively, you can grab people's attention with a piece of music that they recognise. In the 'church in the pub' (see Chapter 10) the talk was introduced either with a video, or with a piece of music that everybody (under 35) would know. An address on the meaning of life began with *Bittersweet Symphony* by The Verve.

In technical terms there are three things to remember:

The first is that your equipment must be top-notch. What sounds good at home, does not necessarily work in a church building which tends to be larger (unless you have a *really* big house). If you have to turn up the volume too loud on a domestic amplifier, the sound distorts. A CD is better than a tape, because it won't wow and flutter. In all cases, *try it out first in the room where you'll be,* before you use it in worship!

The second is that, whatever music you choose, it will not be to everyone's taste. Even if you pick your favourite progressive rock project from the early 70's, there will be some who will not appreciate it. You might think that experimental psychedelia ought to be universally popular, but, disappointingly, it is not.

It's a memo from the church. They don't mind if you play the occasional hymn on your electric guitar; however, they'd rather you didn't play it with your teeth, set it on fire, or smash it at the end of your song.

Classical music is another option, although there are problems here, too. Many well-known classical tunes have already been taken over by the advertising industry. So you can either choose something that is not very familiar, or something that people do know, but then associate with a particular product. You may be asking people to meditate on the goodness of God in creation when all they can think of is deodorant.

The third thing to remember is copyright law. Any professionally pro-

duced music will have a clause prohibiting unauthorised public performance. This means that every time you want to use that classic Blues tape, you will have to ask permission and possibly pay royalties. This is impractical, but the laws ought not to be bent. After all, if you are offering your best to God, this should not include stolen music.

If you do want people to think, then why not choose silence? Just being still is undervalued in most protestant traditions. Often our worship is like fast food eaten on the run. One course must follow another without any gaps, or else we might not have time to fit everything in, and that would be terrible, wouldn't it? – Or would it?

In France, where good cooking is taken seriously, there are often long pauses between the courses to allow people to digest their meal properly. You could allow silences so that people could digest what has happened in the worship before rushing on to the next thing. Silence is nothing to be afraid of. There does not have to be something happening all the time. And the good news is that you don't even have to show out-of-focus slides of the Lake District with it.

Whatever music you choose, make it enjoyable. Your people will remember the songs they sang long after the sermon has been forgotten. Music does matter. Keep your music simple and profound, and don't worry about keeping to a theme. If you can strive for excellence in the music, then you are well on the way with your worship.

Irish Whiskey pudding

4oz Self-raising flour   *4oz Bread crumbs*
4oz Shredded suet   *1 large egg*
Miniature of whiskey   *Tin of treacle*
Fire extinguisher

Mix well together flour, bread crumbs and suet. Add beaten egg until a smooth consistency is formed. Add two tablespoons of the whiskey and mix well in.

Pour as much treacle as you dare into a well-buttered basin. Add the mixture on top. Steam for 2 hours, or microwave on full power for 12 minutes.

Before serving, heat up a ladle half-full of whiskey over ring until boiling. Pour over pudding and set alight. (Cold whiskey will not burn well). Utilise fire extinguisher if things get out of hand.

Serve in the dark with lots of custard.

Serves:	4 people
Calories:	Innumerable
Disclaimer:	Do not drive or operate heavy machinery after eating this pudding.

Chapter 6
Side dishes

Extra items

The traditional three-course meal has a set format and a fixed way of doing things. These days, people are far more flexible and like to have side dishes, maybe a salad, maybe sauces and pickles, maybe a naan bread or vegetable dish. These allow you to cater for the needs and likes of particular individuals at the table.

Today's worship can also have lots of new and different extras. Here are a few of them:

- ☺ Family time
- ☺ Testimony
- ☺ Poetry
- ☺ Meditation
- ☺ Ministry
- ☺ Dance
- ☺ Offering
- ☺ Drama
- ☺ Video

You can add to your worship by including one or more of these elements according to the particular tastes of the congregation. If you are called to lead worship in more than one place, then you can keep the core components the same each time, but use different side dishes to vary the services so that they are tailored to the community. For instance, a less devout group could find drama more helpful than meditation. Look through this chapter and see what things would work in your fellowship.

Family time

God is interested in every part of our lives. With God, you can't pretend that when you are in your Sunday best you are any different from what you are during the week. You bring your experiences, hopes and fears with you when you come to worship. So why not share them with each other?

Family time is an opportunity to do just that. You set apart a few minutes near the start of the service, and ask the congregation about their news, and what is happening in their lives. You give people the chance to speak and to share.

- Sometimes it is good news, for instance when people have a birthday. Don't forget to ask if there is anybody else who has a birthday today, or this week, and include them as well.

- Sometimes the news can be of what God has been doing (see Testimony).

- Sometimes the news can be about what is going on during the week and be a chance to advertise events.

- Sometimes the news can be bad, as in an illness, and be an occasion for prayer.

If you are going to have a Family time, then it is best done week in and week out. A one-off event may just be confusing. Whatever is involved, it is all part of the worship and reminds you that God wants to be in every aspect of your life. And it's better than the traditional listing of 'the notices' to an indifferent and comatose congregation.

How the mood is set

Call to worship *Pastoral prayer* *Special music* *The notices*

Testimony

What is testimony? It is the chance for somebody to say what God has done for *them*, and is one of the most effective means of evangelism, because it speaks directly to your own experience. If somebody ordinary who comes to worship with you can experience God, then so can you.

Testimony must be real. It should be simple and profound. There is no need for embroidery. It also has to be humble. The key feature of testimony is that it says how much God has done for you, rather than what you have done for God. The former glorifies God, the latter is just boasting. The most effective testimony is where God has worked in your life even when you didn't deserve it and not because your love/faith/bank balance is large. Testimony will often replace (or reduce the length of) a sermon.

Both Family time and Testimony can be cringeworthy if they get hijacked by the same person each week. Beware the virtuoso testifier. If you are going to include testimony in your service, it is only fair to ask the people involved beforehand and not to spring it upon them.

Poetry

There are two types of poetry, your own and other people's. To use your own poetry in worship is inappropriate. If your verse is doggerel, then people will cringe. Even if your poetry is brilliant, then maybe you are being self-indulgent.

Worship is about giving the glory to God and not to yourself. Worship is not an excuse to show off how clever you are. If you must share your poetry with God, then be humble enough to share it with God when you are on your own.

I went to a service where the leader used to read out poetry which he had published in a book. He also told us where we could buy it. This was not good worship.

One of the problems with using other people's poetry is that it is not always Christian. There is a sense in which all poetry is religious, in that just as God spoke a world into being from nothing, so a poet speaks a poem into being from nothing. But just because poetry is *religious,* does not mean to say that it is *Christian.* Many poets have sought their own morality and have deliberately fought against Christianity. Great poets are not always humble and great poetry does not always give the glory to God.

I have heard poetry read out in a church meeting which was about the ultimate triumph of the human will. The listeners thought that it was a lovely poem, but Christians do not actually believe that. Christians do believe in the ultimate futility of the human will and the triumph of God's will.

Before you use somebody else's poetry in worship, make absolutely sure that the sentiments being expressed are authentically Christian!

The second problem with using other people's poetry is that it is such a subjective medium. How can you tell whether a poem is any good or not? Do you trust your own judgement? Or do you follow the judgement of critics? There will be plenty of people who will disagree with your opinion. Even if you follow the received wisdom of critics, there is no guarantee that your choices will be popular.

Take Kipling for instance. During his lifetime he was regarded as a brilliant writer and even won the Nobel Prize for Literature. Then, for many years he was looked down upon as an imperialist. Now he has been rehabilitated and is trendy again. So is his poetry good or bad? They are the same poems, so how can they have been good once, then bad, then good again? If 'good' poetry is

what the critics prefer, then this will change over the years, so you may as well choose what you like, because sooner or later it will be fashionable. If 'good' poetry is in the ear of the reader, then you may as well choose what you like anyway, for who is to tell you that their judgement is better than yours? Either way you get to choose. Whether the poetry of your choice is 'lowbrow' or 'highbrow', it is your taste and not the critics' that counts. Worship is not just for the elite.

Critics cannot impose their taste on your private reading, but neither should you impose your tastes on the congregation in public worship. Poetry in worship can be inspiring, but too often it is self-indulgent. You may want to show off that you are Renaissance Man or Woman, but worship is too important for that. If you must use poetry, then try to keep it short, relevant and clear.

The highest forms of poetry

The highest forms of poetry are the limerick and the sonnet*. Anybody can write poetry that doesn't rhyme and just rambles along, but it takes real skill to write a good limerick.

There was a young poet named Ray
whose lifestyle led him to say:
'All my money has gone
on wine, women and song
and the rest I've just frittered away.'

*A sonnet is an extra long limerick, but lacks the sense of humour.

Meditation

Meditation is frowned on in some circles as being dangerous Eastern mysticism. It can be meaningful or embarrassingly uncomfortable. If you are going to lead a meditation with a group who are not used to it, then make it a short one. To be able to meditate is a skill that is picked up with practice. If you make the first example too long, then folk will say, 'Meditation? We tried that, but we didn't like it. It was too difficult'.

Make things simple and easy for your people. Staring at candles while the 'inner depths of your being are cleansed', or looking *through* the icon at the truth revealed beyond' are New-Age ideas, not Christian ones. It would be better to get people to meditate on a verse from the Bible or a particular short prayer, of which one of the most famous is the 'Jesus prayer': 'Jesus, Son of God, have mercy on me, a sinner.' The meditation doesn't have to last for ever and a day. Five minutes will seem an awfully long time, if you have never done it before.

If you do use meditations, don't make them too pretentious. It is not about how clever you are, it is about how good God is. Allow people to concentrate in a quiet, relaxed and friendly atmosphere. Keep distractions to a minimum. This will not be possible if there are a lot of children about, or if people are coughing and spluttering with the 'flu, or if the railway runs past the building. Choose your group, and your time, and your surroundings carefully.

Ministry

A time of ministry allows your people to use their charismatic gifts. Not everyone feels this is appropriate, but in some gatherings people will pray in tongues, pray for one another in groups, have words of knowledge or be slain in the Spirit. If your congregation does this regularly, you will know all about it. If this sounds unusual to you, then maybe you should experience it elsewhere before trying it on your own folks. A less charismatic approach is to reserve a section of the building for people to pray with each other after the service is finished. Even more straightforward is to 'open' the communion rail and announce that folk can come and kneel at the front if they want to pray or be prayed with.

Dance

Dance is becoming more and more popular in worship. It is very visual and theoretically could be moving. So much of what you do in worship is with your mind. Sometimes it is good to use your body. Ideally dance should be able to reach out to people who find a solely intellectual approach off-putting. Dance should be a creative way of reaching new people. It should be able to express simple and profound truths in a new and different way.

Unfortunately, it doesn't always. There is only a limited number of steps available and five minutes of dancing can really begin to drag. It is not long before the dance starts repeating. Dance is very hard to do well. If you do go ahead, don't forget the practicalities, and allow yourself plenty of space. Use sparingly. (See the box)

Seven dance steps

☺ The sweep.
Make a motion with your arms to the left as if you were sweeping leaves.

☺ The seed.
Remember at school when you had to curl up and pretend to be an acorn, then become a tall tree and back again?

☺ The knife.
Clasp your hands to your chest as if you have been stabbed.

☺ The roof's coming down.
On your knees stick your hands in the air as high as you can.

☺ The sweep again, only this time to the right.

☺ The knife again, in case anybody missed it the first time.

☺ Start the whole lot again, this time in slow motion.
(Have we got seven yet?)

Offering

Okay, so maybe the offering isn't that new and different, but it is part of the worship. We offer ourselves to God, and we also offer our money for his use. You can call it an offering, an offertory or a collection; it doesn't matter. It can also happen anywhere in the service, from the beginning to the end. A good tip with the children is to ask for the money early. If you leave it in their pockets, they can start to rattle it or drop it on the floor.

Should you sing a hymn while you take up the offering? That is entirely up to you. Some people don't like it because they can't do two things at once, but you do what you like.

Let's do something religious.
We'll take up a collection
Illustration by Brian Blake

Drama

Now this can be exciting. A picture can paint a thousand words and your creative drama can say all you need to say in just a couple of minutes. There are two main options, each with two branches. Your options are either to use a sketch out of a book or to write your own. The former has the advantage of being tried and tested (allegedly). The latter has the advantage of being free. Most books of sketches ask for a one-off licence fee of some kind. (and *you* wouldn't offer something stolen to God in your worship, would you?)

Once you have decided which option to choose, then your two branches are either true drama, or mime. A true drama has actors who say their lines, while a mime has a narrator who reads from a script and people silently do as they are bidden. This has the great advantage that your actors do not have to learn any lines, which will be very popular when it comes to casting. (It is possible to have a mime without a narrator and everything done in silence, but this is best left to professional buskers in Covent Garden)

It is not that difficult to write a sketch for miming, or even to adapt a Bible story. The parable of the Good Samaritan (Luke 10:30-37) is a good example. You don't need to change the text at all to make an impact. The story can be read straight from the Bible, whilst people mime the actions. Children in particular love taking part, especially as it is a story containing action and violence. Even the moral doesn't need to be explained as the parable ends with the words: 'You go and do the same.'

If you feel confident enough to write your own sketch, then remember the quality of your setting and the quality of your actors. If your sketch requires five different scenes including Castle Dracula and the bridge of the Starship Enterprise, it may be difficult to organise over a half-term weekend. Similarly, if your leading actress needs to learn a 5,000 word soliloquy and to stare at the audience with a defiant, and yet tragically vulnerable look of awe, you may have problems filling the rôle. Cut your coat according to your cloth.

If you do write your own sketch, remember the warnings in the poetry section. Worship is not about proving what a great actor you could have been if only you had had the breaks. Nor is it about being pretentious. Let your drama glorify God, not the playwright.

Finally, less is more. The shorter your sketch, the more impact it will have. Cut out all the extra details that obscure your main point. Ideally, it should require very little explanation, either beforehand or afterwards. If you have to say, 'The knight in shining armour represented the figure of wisdom battling against unbelief', then you've lost the plot. Let your drama stand on its own.

Video

It is possible to do work with a camcorder very easily and comparatively cheaply these days. As with poetry and drama, there are two types of video, your own and other people's.

During the week before, you can shoot your own video and edit it for use. You could interview people in the streets to find out who people thought that Jesus was. When you hear the answers, they might be a spur to evangelism! You could video areas in your neighbourhood that require prayer. You could video your own drama, or music, or whatever.

If you were working in a team and not everyone was available at the same time, some members could make their contribution on video.

Commercial video, that is, other people's work, can be used to introduce a theme. A snippet from a well-known television series can engage the interest and then be followed by a relevant talk. At the church in the pub (See Chapter 10), a clip from an episode of *The Simpsons* was particularly effective. Don't forget the copyright laws (see Chapter 12).

Other items

Worship is the offering of ourselves to God. With this in mind, there is no limit to what we can bring and use. Let your imagination run loose!

Yorkshire Pudding

8oz Plain flour   *Pint of milk*
2oz fat   *Pinch of salt*
2 large eggs

Sieve the flour and salt into a large mixing bowl. Make a well in the centre of the flour, and add the eggs until a smooth consistency is formed. Add the milk and beat hard. If desired, use half milk and half water. Let this batter mixture sit for twenty minutes.

Meanwhile, put the fat (traditionally beef dripping) into a baking tin and pop it in the oven. Beat the mixture well for a further five minutes, then remove the baking tin which should now be smoking hot. Quickly pour in the batter and return to the oven for 30 minutes at Gas Mark 7, 425F, 220C.

Serve with gravy as a filling starter, or as a side dish.

Chapter 7

Special meals

Special services

There are some special meals, when we like to be more formal, and make an occasion of them. These include Christmas lunch, graduation dinners, wedding receptions and funeral ham teas. We use these meals to celebrate important times and to mark the changing stages of life.

Unsurprisingly, the Church has special services as well. These services are used to celebrate the important times in our lives. Pagan religions had celebrations of 'rites of passage'. The Church took these over and 'Christianised' them.

Here are some guidelines that you may find helpful when you are requested to take part.

Baptism

Anybody can do a baptism. In extreme circumstances, in hospitals, nurses have stepped in to do baptisms when there has been no minister available. The only necessities are baptising with water, and using the words 'I baptise you, (name), in the name of the Father and of the Son and of the Holy Spirit', although in the Acts of the Apostles, people were simply baptised in the name of Jesus. Their baptism was valid.

In the early Church, there were some people who thought that only a worthwhile person could do a worthwhile baptism. A very famous Christian called St Augustine argued against them, that baptism did not depend upon the human with the water, but upon God with the Spirit. St Augustine's view prevailed, and that is what the entire Church believes today. Most institutional churches assume the minister will perform the baptisms.

However, the Church is not agreed on whether people should be baptised as children or as adults. Some denominations believe that we should baptise children as a sign of God's grace, that God loves us even before we are aware of it. Other denominations believe that you should only be baptised when you are old enough to know what you are doing, and when you can make your own confession of faith. There are (sometimes heated!) arguments on both sides. Theologically, you can only be baptised once.

Onlookers were amazed as it took escape artist Joe only 15 minutes to escape from his baptism.

© Gospel Films, Inc. – www.reverendfun.com

It is absolutely essential to speak to the parents first before any infant baptism as they may want their children to make up their own minds when they are grown up. In all but the most urgent of circumstances, baptisms will be performed by the minister or church leader.

Many churches have preparation classes for those who wish to be baptised, or for the parents of infants.

Dedication

A dedication service is an alternative to infant baptism. The new life of a baby is celebrated, but without the actual baptismal rite. This keeps the celebration, but allows the child to make their own mind up about baptism at a later stage.

You can do a dedication service in the home, in a hall, or in your usual place of worship. There is much more flexibility, and you could write your own service. The basic elements are of thanksgiving for a new life, with all the potential that brings, and of 'dedicating' the baby to God. In other words, to offer this new life back to the God who has given it. The parents make some kind of commitment to raise the child in a Christian home.

Entry into the Church

For those Churches which practise adult baptism, entry to the church will be in the context of a service with total immersion in water.

For those Churches which practise infant baptism, there is a service of confirmation, where adults *confirm* the promises that were made on their behalf when they were children.

Wedding

Contrary to popular belief, anybody can *perform* a wedding ceremony in England as long as the right people are there to *witness* what goes on. Within the Roman Catholic and Anglican churches only the priest can officiate, but elsewhere anybody can lead the service.

Because a wedding is the making of a legal contract there are restrictions. Weddings must take place in a registered building (often a church) and in the presence of an authorised person (often the minister) between the hours of 8am and 6pm. As long as the authorised person *hears* the legal words being spoken by the couple, the wedding is valid. Theoretically, somebody else can lead the worship.

When the registered building is not a place of worship, but a hotel or a stately home, then the ceremony *must not contain any religious element whatsoever.* Even a poem which mentions God is not allowed.

Marriages are not to be taken lightly at all and you should neither enter into one, *nor perform one* without knowing exactly what you are doing! Once again, the minister or Church leader will usually take the service. Most institutional churches assume the minister will perform the weddings, because of the legal responsibilities involved.

Seven wedding myths

✠ You have to have bridesmaids

✠ You have to have a best man

✠ The father has to give away the bride

✠ The bride must wear white

✠ The bride must have a bouquet

✠ The bride must promise to obey

✠ You have to sing *All things bright and beautiful*

Wedding blessing

A wedding blessing takes place after the Register Office has performed the legal ceremony. Because the couple are already married, you do not have to worry about the technicalities, apart from seeing the marriage certificate.

Some denominations will not marry those who have been divorced, but they will offer a wedding blessing. You can devise your own service and celebrate the joining together of two people. The blessing can take place any time after the legal wedding, maybe many years later. A couple could become Christians twenty years after their secular wedding and want a blessing.

You could also be asked to bless a ring, or to commemorate a silver wedding anniversary. Under such circumstances you can perform a simple but dignified ceremony, with some elements of thanksgiving and rededication.

Funeral

Anybody can perform a funeral in the protestant Church. Occasionally ministers will miss a funeral, and, if they cannot be found, then the undertakers have to act in their place. This is not ideal, but these things happen. Nowadays it is becoming more common for families to create and perform their own service. You may be asked to help.

Key issues would be dignity, simplicity and honesty. Emotions will be running high, and previously capable people may find it very hard to stand up and speak in front of others. If you are going to lead, then make sure you can do it without breaking down. Funerals can be pastorally complex and professional clergy receive training on the issues involved. Be very careful not to get out of your depth!

Sometimes there can be a **memorial service** after the burial or cremation. At such times an element of thanksgiving would be in order.

Burial of ashes can also be requested. A very short service is all that is needed. There does not have to be a repeat of the funeral service.

Communion

Now this really is where there are differences between the denominations. They even have different names for the sharing of bread and wine. The Roman Catholic Church and the Orthodox Churches teach that only an ordained man can perform the Mass. The Anglican Church teaches that an ordained man or woman can perform the Eucharist. The Methodist Church teaches that anybody can do Communion, *but* for the sake of church order restricts it to ordained men and women and those who have received a special dispensation from the annual Conference. The Baptist and United Reformed Churches allow their elders to do communion. The Salvation Army does not have communion at all. House Churches and other unstructured denominations *usually* allow anybody to do communion. (And if they don't, you can always start your own!)

In some traditions, the communion service will be the main form of worship, and if you are not ordained, you are unlikely to be asked to lead. All churches take communion seriously and have rules about who can preside. Make sure you know those rules.

An alternative to a communion is the **love feast**. This was a feature of the early Church and the eighteenth century revival, and is appropriate when there is no ordained person available. To make sure there is absolutely no confusion with communion, tea is used instead of wine and crackers or biscuits instead of bread. Often done in the context of a meal (cooking up worship indeed), the love feast encourages fellowship, sharing and testimony.

Ordination

An ordination service recognises a special calling to ministry. Different churches have different names for these rôles, including deacons, elders, presbyters, priests, bishops and even archbishops. Ordination usually involves the 'laying on of hands' by those previously ordained to show a continuation of tradition and calling.

Less formal, but no less important is a **commissioning service**. This is an act of worship to set aside members of the Church for special tasks. This could be for work amongst young people, for preaching, or for being a worship leader.

Healing service

There is controversy over the subject of healing. Some people say that the gift was only for the time of the Apostles. Others say that healing takes place today. One of the fears about healing services is that they can cause more damage than they are worth. If people are made to feel that their lack of healing is down to their lack of faith, then they will suffer terrible guilt. They will think that their suffering is their own fault. The life of Jesus and the Apostles shows that suffering does come even to those who have faith. St Paul had a thorn in the flesh that would not go away.

Healing can come in varied ways. Sometimes that healing is not physical but spiritual, as people learn to cope with their suffering. At other times, there can be a 'healing of the memories', where a past hurt is seen in a new light. Then there is the healing of emotions, when anger or grief find comfort.

There are occasions when healing can come in unexpected ways. One man I know had a heart attack the night after a healing service. Fortunately, it was only a minor one, and he was told to regard it as a warning. He changed his lifestyle and his diet, and ten years later was still going strong. The 'healing' came through the heart attack: God moves in mysterious ways, his wonders to perform.

We do not really understand suffering, nor do we really understand healing. Whoever leads such a service should be sensitive to the feelings of all people present.

Carol service

People who do not come to church still feel it belongs to them, and that they should have a say in how things are run. This attitude often shows itself at the time of the year outsiders think of as 'the most Christian'. There is a strong demand for Christmas carol services to follow a traditional pattern. People have favourite carols that they expect to sing.

This goes to the heart of the issue of worship. You can decide that people are all wrong, and that you are going to give them what you think they *should* have. *They* might want traditional carols and readings, but you are going to give them what is good for them. The advantage of this approach is that they won't be back next year to complain again.

Or, you can accept the taste of the people for a traditional service and use that format to get across your message.

It could be the one chance you have to make an impact on many of the people in the congregation. Why not concentrate on taking that chance?

Remembrance service

In Britain, Remembrance services take place on the nearest Sunday to 11 November, the Armistice Day in the First World War.

Once again, there are traditional expectations and the chance to speak to people who are only in church rarely. This is not the occasion for your theories on how war could be ended if only people were a little bit nicer to each other.

If you are not a preacher, then give the opportunity to somebody who is. If you are a preacher, then remember that you are a preacher of the Gospel and not of the nation. You are there to give God's word on a solemn day, not to glorify this country's victories in the past.

You can make Remembrance Sunday meaningful by making this personal. In the church in Liverpool we discovered a record book from 1916 and read out a list of the thirty Sunday school teachers from our church out on active service.

Thanksgiving service

You may be asked to do a service outside your normal place of worship. This could be to celebrate the opening of a new building or to commemorate the anniversary of a particular event, or it could be a big civic occasion.

In such circumstances, your usual resources may not be available. Just as you cannot do as much with a picnic as you can in your own kitchen, so your options are limited when you have to take everything with you for worship.

Brevity is a virtue. It may also be a good idea not to use music, unless everybody can have a copy of the words and enough people will know the hymns. Alternatively, take your own musicians or singers with you to give a very strong lead.

In all cases, keep things short and simple.

Blessing of a home

This is a tricky one. It does not really make much sense to bless bricks and mortar, and yet people can be very keen to have it done. Some people see it as a kind of insurance policy, while others just feel the need for some kind of comfort in a place to which they have moved. Either way, a very short act of worship is all that you need.

It gives you the opportunity to meet people in their own homes and to worship with them. You might even suggest that they like to continue the process by praying each day.

Exorcism

Exorcism can be related to a call for a blessing of a home, if the reason for the request is 'things that go bump in the night'. This is a dangerous area, and one not to be meddled with by those who do not know what they are doing. If you believe in the demonic, then you are dealing with evil, and if you do not believe in the demonic, then you are dealing with serious mental illness. Both should be left to the experts.

Your Anglican Diocese will have an official exorcist. Pass any enquiries directly to them.

School assemblies

See the advice given in chapter 9.

Blessing of the animals

The old dictum: 'Never work with children or animals' holds true for worship. If you are called upon to do a service that involves 'blessing of the animals', then know that the chances are that it won't go exactly to plan.

Traditional Christmas Lunch

Vegetable soup
Roast turkey
Roast potatoes
Mashed potatoes
Brussels sprouts
Carrots
Peas
Cabbage
Buttered parsnips
Stuffing
Bread sauce
Cranberry sauce
Gravy
Christmas pudding

It's not surprising people feel like
sleeping afterwards!

Chapter 8

Practical tips ——————————

—————————— # Helpful hints

This chapter is full of simple ideas to make your presentation palatable for your hearers.

How do I start?

If you were making a meal, the first thing you should do would be to wash your hands. The religious equivalent of this is saying a prayer.

These days, hygiene is a real concern for all cooks, and they are advised to wash their hands after working with meat or fish, after using a rubbish bin, after handling money and even after touching their hair or mouth. The idea is to keep hands clean at all times, and to make washing hands a habit. If in doubt, wash your hands.

In the same way, you should make prayer a habit. If in doubt – say a prayer. All your preparations and organisation should be steeped in prayer. This is not somehow to make you 'clean', but to offer all that you do to God.

What should I wear?

The simple answer to this is 'wear what everybody else does'. If the people you are meeting with wear jeans and t-shirts, then do the same. If the people

you are leading wear clothes for business, then do the same. If the people you are worshipping with wear their Sunday best, then do the same. You are trying to direct people's attention towards God and away from yourself, so don't wear anything that will get in the way.

Brian the Bull liked to look unobtrusive when leading worship

© Gospel Films, Inc. – www.reverendfun.com

If you are not an ordained member of the clergy, then do not dress up as if you are. If your church does have people who are set aside to be ministers, or priests, or whatever, then you are trying to give yourself a status you do not have. If your church does not believe in liturgical vestments, then you won't want to wear robes. Either way you should dress normally. Never pretend you are somebody else.

Follow the example of Jesus who wore ordinary clothes and yet spoke with authority. The effectiveness of your worship comes from you having something important to say rather than having something important to wear.

How should I speak?

Speaking in public is all about clarity. You do not have to be too loud, you do not have to shout, but you do have to be clear. It is no use having something to say, if what you say is not heard.

There are different techniques involved in speaking with and without a microphone. Unfortunately, there is no substitute for experience, and no easy way of gaining that experience without standing up and speaking in front of a crowd. People in general have two major fears. One is dying and the other is speaking in public. It is possible to do both at the same time.

A helpful tip is to practice by going into an empty room (preferably the place where you are going to speak, although this is not always possible) and getting somebody to listen to you and make comments. Even then, an empty room is very different from a room with a crowd of expectant listeners.

Speaking in public is different from speaking in private. If you speak normally, then it will be too quiet for everybody else, and too fast, especially if you are nervous. If your public speaking sounds slow and loud to you, then it should sound about right to your listeners.

When you are using a microphone, don't forget to turn it off during the singing, or you will drown out everybody.

Look your audience in the eye. Don't stare off into space. And smile rather than frown!

Who should I be?

You should be yourself, because that is what God wants you to be in worship. God does not want you to pretend to be somebody else. Don't try and imitate somebody else's style, even if you admire them. If you are no good at telling jokes, then you would be ill-advised to use them just because the minister does. If you use your hands a lot when you speak normally, then keep on doing it at the front. If you are normally thoughtful, then let this shine through. There is no right or wrong way to be, but you do want to be yourself. God chose you, so who are you to say that God is wrong?

What should I write down?

To start with, you should write down everything. This does not mean to say that you have to read out what you have written, but it does mean that if you get flustered, your notes will be right there. Like actors who have learnt their lines, you could be word perfect, but still need a prompt when the actual performance comes. Having a full script means that you are ready for any eventuality.

When should I arrive?

You should arrive as early as possible. You will have rehearsed what you want to say beforehand. You will have your full script. You will have copies of what you are doing for the musicians (if there are any), for the stewards or sidespeople (if they need to put hymn numbers up) and for any other participants, so that they know when they are needed.

Then you will take the time to test the microphone, the acoustics and the surroundings. You will also discover if anything is missing, for instance they might have a different hymnbook from the one you were expecting, or you might need an electrical extension cord for your amplifier.

If you arrive early, you can sort these things out, without getting in a panic. Then you can have a considered time of prayer to calm yourself. If you arrive late, you are banking on everything working first time. Life isn't like that, *so get there early.*

The story is told of the young minister who turned up at the last minute for a service in a very liturgical church. There was something very wrong with the amplification system, so he said, 'There seems to be something wrong with this microphone'.

The reply came from the congregation, 'And also with you'.

Opposition

You will not be expecting hecklers. If you are expecting trouble, then maybe somebody more experienced should be called upon to lead. Otherwise, smile sweetly and keep going! Sometimes people will come in late and make a disturbance, or a child will start to cry. Allow time for people to get settled again.

How to handle meat

Hands should be washed before and after handling meat to avoid cross-contamination.

Different knives should be used for raw and cooked meats.

Cooked meat should always be stored above raw meat in the fridge.

Meat should be cooked enough so that it is hot all the way through. Make sure any juices are clear rather than pink.

Chapter 9

Children's meals ———

——— Children's services and all-age worship

For some reason, children always seem to eat different meals from adults. Just when you want to settle down to a nice quiet meal, with sophisticated conversation and good company, the children barge in and want to eat chips and sauce, noisily, messily and unpleasantly. It is even worse if they are teenagers, because then they want to eat on their own, when they like and not with the family, because it's boring.

So it is in church. You want to settle down in an atmosphere of calm and peace and stillness, when the children barge in and make lots of noise, lots of mess and want to be entertained. It is even worse if they are teenagers, because they don't want to come to church with the family at all, because it's boring. This gives you four options as strategies for coping:

1. Keep adults and children separate.

2. Make the children behave like adults.

3. Let the adults behave like children.

4. Make the worship 'work' for both adults and children.

Keeping adults and children separate is the easiest option. To keep everybody happy, the adults have their own food, and the children have beans and chips and dinosaur burgers at a different table, so that they can make a mess. In church terms this would imply that the adults have their own diet of grown-up stuff and the children have their diet specially made for them next door. This has the *advantage* of tailoring worship to the taste of each group, but the *disadvantage* of never meeting together.

Seven ages of drink

☺ Birth: Milk

☺ Aged 5: Cola

☺ Aged 15: Cider

☺ Aged 20: Beer

☺ Aged 30: Chardonnay

☺ Aged 50: Single malt Scotch

☺ Aged 80+: Milk

The adults' food is sophisticated and clever, which is why they learn about God while listening to a sermon. The children's food has to be both tasty and nourishing, which is why they learn about God while drawing pictures. The trouble is that this way they never learn about God from each other. The adults miss out on 'Unless you come as a little child you will not enter the Kingdom of Heaven'. The children miss out on any experience of adult worship and find it alien when they grow up.

Seven ages of Church

☺ Birth: Listening to the sermon and crying.

☺ Aged 5: Listening to the sermon while drawing pictures.

☺ Aged 15: Listening to the sermon while thinking about the redhead on the third row.

☺ Aged 20: Listening to the sermon and wondering what it's about.

☺ Aged 30: Listening to the sermon and thinking you could do better.

☺ Aged 50: Listening to the sermon and knowing that you could do better.

☺ Aged 80+: Listening to the sermon and remembering that it used to be better.

Children should be given a taste of what the adults have in order to whet their appetite. Then we can say to them, 'When you grow up, you'll be able to have this all the time . . . ' (Whether this is a threat or a promise is up to you.)

The second option is to force the children to behave, on your adult terms. They are to be quiet, they are to be well behaved, they are to be little adults. They are to eat with you and they are to worship with you. Failure to comply with the rules leads to expulsion and possibly being sent to bed.

This option only works with biddable children and strong-willed adults. It can lead to conflict, both at the dinner table and in church, and can leave everybody disgruntled. Worst of all, it gives the impression of church as something to be endured rather than enjoyed, an impression which leads many children to leave once they are teenagers. Clever children soon realise that if they make enough fuss, they get to go out and play with the toys. This may involve some initial chastisement, but is well worth it.

Many churches have a policy of forcing children to behave like adults, without realising it. They would love to see children in the service, and don't understand where they've gone. Then when any children do appear, they expect them to be silent or else they tell them off. Later they wonder, 'Why don't they come any more?'

The third option is to offer the adults the chance to behave on the same terms as the children. Adults love the opportunity to be young again and eat jelly and ice cream and crisps. Many a preacher has discovered that the sermon is long forgotten while the children's talk remains. This option only works with tolerant adults who care that the children enjoy the service more than they care about being fed with 'serious worship'.

Many churches have a hybrid of options one, two and three. They have the children and the adults together at the start of the service. They sing an exciting song, then ask everyone to sit down and be still for a quiet prayer. The children are expected to behave like adults during the prayers while their parents try to keep them silent.

Then the adults are expected to behave like kids during the 'children's talk'. Afterwards, both groups go their separate ways.

If that kind of worship were a meal, you would have all kinds of problems. You would start off making a lot of noise and having a lot of fun. Then you would expect the kids to eat their soup in absolute silence, followed by the adults sharing in the kids' jelly and ice cream. Finally, you would split the group up and eat separate meals. If the church is supposed to be the family of God, then I'm afraid this family sounds dysfunctional!

Instead, while the children are there, make sure that everything suits them. If the children are happy in church, then the parents will keep coming. Ensure that the music is suitable for them. If this means the adults doing action songs, then *so be it*. Ensure the prayers are suitable too. Once the children are gone, you can move to a more adult style of worship.

Children will start to fidget when they are bored, and they will show their displeasure by making noise. Adults (having been taught to be polite) are less likely to leave spinach and sprouts on their plates and say, 'I don't like it!' In the same way, adults are less likely to start talking and fidgeting and crawling about during the service (in theory).

However, the fourth and best option is to make the worship work for both children and adults at the same time. If the service is exciting enough, then the children will enjoy it. If the service is deep enough then the adults will enjoy it.

Children's talk

Talking to the children is difficult. You shouldn't be patronising (like the preacher who came down from the high pulpit saying 'Let me come down to your level'). Nor should you be trivial. There is an art to telling stories. If you haven't got it, then why not bring along somebody else who has?

If you cannot do that, then leave out the children's talk altogether, but make the first part of the service so exciting that you don't need one. Better no children's talk at all than a cringeworthy one.

Simplistic worship will not be enough for the adults. Complicated worship will leave the children bored. Simple and profound worship will be appropriate for both. It *is* possible.

Your example can come from the world of television. The ideal audience for a television station is children watching with their parents, because then their viewing figures are maximised, and their advertising and thus their income is at its most lucrative. Children have their own shows, but if you can get the adults to watch with them, then you start to make serious money. The most successful shows work on more than one level. The most successful worship has to work on more than one level, too.

Take *The Simpsons* for instance. At one level it is a children's show with lots of action and slapstick. At another level it is a sophisticated satire on the

American way of life. Children and adults can watch together. Both enjoy the show, but for different reasons.

Or take the *Banana Splits*. I watched the show as a child and loved the humour. Seeing a show recently as an adult, I realised how subversive and counter-cultural it was, something that had gone way over my head when I was younger.

You may not like the underlying message propagated by these television shows, but whether you like it or not, their message is being communicated well.

Television companies spend fortunes trying to find this magic formula of appealing to both children and adults at the same time, and you do not have the wealth of talent that they do. But at least you now know what you are aiming for, worship that is simple and profound and material that works on several levels.

Providentially, the Bible and in particular the parables of Jesus do work on several levels. The Bible is full of characters who stand by themselves and don't need lengthy explanation and which can be appreciated by young and old alike. The story of Moses and the plagues of Egypt is loved by children (all those boils and gnats and frogs and the bloodthirstiness) whilst adults can appreciate the wider theme of liberation from slavery of all kinds.

Working with children of a wide age range is hard work. Working with both adults and children is harder. If you are capable of doing it, then you will be an asset to any church. The ideal is worship that works on more than one level.

If you cannot make that ideal, then work with the children. *Cater for the children first and hope that the adults like it too.*

Children need involvement in a way that adults do not. Adults are prepared to sit and watch, but children want to interact. They want to shout things out and do things and participate and get involved.

There are resources to help you. Some churches follow a scheme like *S.A.L.T., Living Stones* or *Partners in Learning*, where the adults and children look at material together. You will find the details in Chapter 12.

All-age worship

Also sometimes known as a family service. This is option three for the whole of the time allocated.

A variation on this is the **parade service**, where uniformed organisations come to worship. You may have to take their flags and prop them up at the front. This is even harder work than a family service because many of the young people will not be used to coming to church. Make that extra effort to make it fun.

Assemblies

School assemblies can be the hardest work of all. In church, you know what *you* are there for, and the children know what *they* are there for. You are on home territory. Even if there are visitors, they expect you to talk about God and Jesus and things like that.

In school it is different. The children can be from many different backgrounds and you have to be sensitive. Children from the Jewish, Moslem and Hindu communities may be in assembly, and may not be expecting Christian worship.

Your job is to be authentically Christian, and yet sensitive to other faiths. You should not go for the lowest common denominator and talk about how everybody sees God the same way, because that is not true. On the other hand, you can't tell them that they are heathens who need to see the light or else.

What you should do is talk about Jesus, how he is exciting, how he is different, and how he is important. You can tell the stories of Jesus and what he means to you without being insensitive. In church you might say, 'We believe that Jesus is the Son of God'. In assembly you might say, 'Christians believe that Jesus is the Son of God'.

The difference is small, but in assembly you are allowing for the fact that children or teachers or parents might have differing views. You can be true to yourself and what you believe without implying that anybody who disagrees with you is a liar.

Don't be afraid to talk about Jesus, because that is what you are there for. It was the witness of Christians and the stories of Jesus that led to the conversion of the multi-faith Roman Empire. Working in a world with other religions is nothing new for the Christian faith. The Church can stand, prosper and grow in such an environment. The problem is that since the time of the Crusades, Christianity has been spread by military conquest. It is hardly surprising that other religions regard us with fear and resentment.

So, be sensitive. Also, be entertaining. This may be some children's only experience of Christian worship. Simple and profound worship can reach out. You can make a difference.

Peas on toast

1oz Plain flour   *1oz Butter*
Half a pint of milk   *8oz Frozen peas*
Salt and pepper to taste *4 Slices of bread*

Put the peas in a pan of salted water and boil for five minutes.

In the meantime, melt the butter in a pan and stir in the flour to make a smooth paste. Keep the heat on and gradually add the milk, stirring all the time to stop lumps forming. Bring to the boil and simmer until it starts to thicken.

Drain the peas and stir them into the mixture and put on a low heat for five minutes.

Toast the bread on both sides and if you like, use butter. Pour on the hot mixture and serve immediately. Add salt and pepper to taste.

Serves: 2-4 children
Calories: Medium

Chapter 10

The proof of the pudding

Real life examples

Easington Village Chapel, County Durham, England

It is all very well reading a cookbook, but what people want to know is do the recipes actually work? It is all very well reading these ideas on worship, but do they really work in practice?

The proof of the pudding is in the eating. Here is the story of Easington Village Chapel in County Durham in the North East of England. Easington Village lies eleven miles south of Sunderland and is a former mining community, although there has been a settlement there since Saxon times. The only English Pope, Nicholas Brakespear, was Rector of Easington in the twelfth century.

There had been a Methodist presence in Easington for more than 150 years. The present building was erected by the Wesleyans in 1870. A small side-room was added in 1961. I arrived as the minister in 1992. By 1994 the cause was collapsing. Mr Lamb was 90 years old. He and Mrs Lamb had been running the church for 61 years. Things were coming to a head.

Worship took place at 3 o'clock every Sunday afternoon, with a regular congregation of between five and seven. The bills could be paid (just) and the building could be maintained (just), but new life was needed. The traditional worship style just did not seem to appeal to the community around.

I wrote a paper offering suggestions about what could be done. I circulated this as widely as possible within the churches of the area. The paper suggested that the church could be sold off to another denomination; it could be made into a residential youth centre; a team of volunteers could revive it; or it could be closed.

Six members of the Methodist Church at nearby Peterlee offered to come over and help. They wanted the chance to do something new, and Easington Village offered that opportunity. The existing members were prepared to relinquish their authority and let the people coming across have free rein.

The old Church last met on Palm Sunday 1994 and had a closing service. The new Church first met on Easter Sunday, but a lot of preparation had taken place that week. The transformation of the premises had been extensive. Work had been done on the building to provide central heating and seat cushions. The church and side-room were painted. (Two years later the side-room would be extended, and built in such a way that a further storey could be added at a later date.)

The transformation of the congregation was far-reaching. The original members of Easington Village kept coming. The new members from Peterlee kept coming. Most encouraging of all, though, were the new people who started attending.

Children from the locality appeared in large numbers. People came from round about who had heard of this experiment in worship, and stayed. Couples with children started coming. Baptisms started to happen again. Weddings began again for the first time in decades, and in 1995 the building became registered for the performance of marriages after 125 years. Four years later congregations had risen to forty adults and fifteen children each Sunday, with continuing growth anticipated.

Change in the worship

The biggest transformation came in the worship. It was clear that people were just not interested in coming to traditional worship. They were voting with their feet. Tired old hymns and tired old worship were driving them away. Something had to change.

The service time was moved to 10.45am. Instead of the preacher leading the worship, the people did. Four volunteers took it in turn to lead the worship in pairs. They chose the opening three or four choruses from *Mission Praise*. Often they were not the ones that I would have chosen, *but that was the point*. The worship leaders knew better than I did with all my ministerial training. They chose music appro-

priate to the congregation and the service. Then the congregation would sit down to sing their prayer chorus: *All my life, Lord, to you I want to give.*

This would be followed by the prayers, a complete mixture of thanksgiving, adoration, confession and intercession as the Spirit led, and usually included the Lord's Prayer. Technically they might not have been in the 'right' order, but they were heartfelt. One of the members would sing a solo and play his guitar and there would be the offering. Then there would be one more song. After all this 'worship' would come the 'preaching', where the children would leave for their own meeting and the selected preacher of the day would give a sermon to those who remained. One more song, sometimes chosen by the preacher, would finish the service.

When I was preaching, every third week, the sermon would be exactly the same as in my other churches. The other congregations continued to shrink in numbers whilst Easington Village grew. Obviously it was not my sermons that were making the difference.

What was distinctive about Easington Village was the congregation-led worship. They were the ones who were making the difference, not me. They were the ones who were leading worship in a style relevant to today. They were the ones who went beyond the old way of doing things in order to create something new. They decided that the 'Sunday lunch – take it or leave it' model was no good at all. The worship did not need to be structured, but it did need to be good. Sometimes they had the theme of the sermon in advance, sometimes they didn't. But either way they could be trusted to do the right thing and create worship that people could enjoy.

The sermons were the same as ever. The music was good, the congregation enjoyed it, because it was modern, and because the musicians were good. In particular the keyboard player, a local lad, was excellent and was paid accordingly. The prayers were good in that they were straightforward and expressed the prayers of the people rather than the latest theological fashion. There was rarely a 'children's talk', but the children enjoyed the part of the service they were in because it was good enough for them too.

People came, and continue to come, because they *enjoy the worship*. Easington Village is like a restaurant that for years had been cooking up the same meals with a shrinking clientele. Now it has new cooks, working together, and making something new, which is pulling people in.

It can be done. You can do it too. What's holding you back?

The Upper Room

The proof of the pudding is in the eating. Here is the story of the Upper Room in Liverpool, a church plant in a pub.

Liverpool city centre had two cathedrals, a pier-head, shopping and nightclubs galore, but a shortage of churches. This didn't matter while the area was empty, but in the early 1990s, people started moving back in.

There had been a Methodist presence in the city centre of Liverpool since the very earliest days. The successful Elm Hall Drive Church was a plant itself from a Methodist Chapel on Grove Street, now the University examination hall. Methodist Central Hall, on Renshaw Street, was a major attraction but closed and became a bar complex. Nearby inner city churches closed and amalgamated over the years.

Other denominations such as the Church of Scotland closed their buildings, and St Luke's, the Anglican Church, was bombed during the war and never reopened. The churches abandoned the centre.

The reason for this flight from the city centre was straightforward. The congregations left. In common with most British cities, the centre became depopulated as people headed for the suburbs. Former houses became offices and shops, former schools were amalgamated and closed down, and former churches were deconsecrated. Even the Central Hall, which drew its congregation from all over the city, saw numbers fall. The city centre became a place full of thousands of people during the daytime, all of who commuted in, but did their shopping, living and worshipping in the suburbs or in Cheshire. Under these circumstances, it made sense for the churches to withdraw, and to consider how to do things on weekdays to attract the office worker and the shopper. They came up with the idea of 'Mission in the Economy', and work with chaplains to the shopworkers.

But in the nineties something different happened. Against all expectations, Liverpool city centre began to be repopulated again.

There were several reasons for this:

1. The Yuppie boom of the eighties. In Liverpool this was centred around the Albert Dock and similar waterfront properties. Many of these people only lived there Monday to Friday, but the point was made, it was possible to live in the city, with all the benefits of convenience and transport.

2. The demand for new housing and the lack of available land. There was pressure on all local authorities to release land for housing. There was pressure from the other side to keep greenbelts and the countryside. Thus, developing 'brownfield' sites (derelict land that had been built on before) in the centre kept everybody happy.

3. European money. Liverpool received substantial funding for urban regeneration, much of which was spent on housing.

4. The universities. As the education sector continued to expand, the universities built more accommodation. Purpose-built suburban halls were both prohibitively expensive and difficult to site. The city centre answered all these problems.

These trends looked set to continue. There would be new housing being built in Liverpool city centre throughout the nineties and beyond.

What was needed was a worshipping community, meeting on a Sunday, attractive to young adults and having a message relevant for today. There was a real gap, a real no-man's-land, a real empty space in the middle of the city. Five years before that had made sense, because there was a gap in the population too. Now, there were thousands of people living in the centre, without a church to serve them. It was decided to plant a Church.

Church planting works, because it releases people to new things. You cannot put new wine in old wine skins. Our present-day Church structure is like an old wine skin – if God pours the new wine of the kingdom in, it will split and crack and break. Where there is a tradition, a set way of doing things, an established order, then it is very difficult to bring in new and exciting worship. It is hard to cater for the outsider, because everything is arranged for the benefit of the insider, from the music, the worship, the building to the structure and organisation.

A new Church can start from scratch and gear everything to its mission. New Churches grow faster than established Churches because they are more flexible. Ministers in their first and second appointments see the greatest numerical growth because they have not been caught up in the 'churchy' culture. New Churches can be all things to all people, in order to win some.

A group of nine volunteers came together to start the new Church. They had the qualities of enthusiasm and commitment, but also many fears and worries. Fortunately they took to the task straight away.

The first step was to find a venue in the centre, and the team came up with a pub called the Florin and Firkin. This was ideally sited next to Lime Street station. Even better, it had a function room upstairs, where the 'church' could meet. It would only cost us £20 a week, and if it didn't work out we could walk away. How much easier than having an ancient building to maintain, although the pub was listed Grade 2.

The name 'The Upper Room' came quickly as it was both geographically accurate and also hinted at the Last Supper. The team deliberately avoided the use of the word 'church' in the title and the word 'Methodist' on the publicity as they thought they added little and could even be counter-productive.

Since the meetings were going to be in a pub, one of the team suggested that, instead of handing out pieces of paper, the publicity should be on beer-mats. Ten thousand were printed. The internet was also used to try to advertise to the young people of Liverpool.

It was decided that there was no point in providing a traditional worship service, and that something more akin to a 'presentation of the Gospel' would be appropriate. There would be elements of a 'normal' church service, but not necessarily in the usual order.

The service started at 11.30am and began with music. The musicians (one keyboard, three guitars, a 'cello and a flute) played three or four upbeat 'praise' songs that people could sing along to if they wanted. There were no books, everything went on the overhead projector. People sat around on the bar stools. Some sang, some lis-tened, some talked. That was fine.

Then either a song from the charts or a video was played (the pub had a licence for sound and vision – see Chapter 5). This would link in with the following short Bible reading and brief talk (ten minutes).

The response to the 'sermon' was to cut out headlines from the day's news-papers to stick on a prayer-board at the front. This exercise did not happen in silence and people could discuss what had been said.

Finally there was one more song, and then the pint glass was passed round for the collection. The whole service lasted for just forty-five minutes. People could stay after to chat, or to go downstairs for something to eat and drink in the pub's main bar.

The team led the worship and the 'sermon' was kept short. People came because they enjoyed the worship and because it was easy to come. It didn't last very long; you could come in and out; you could melt into the crowd; you didn't have to be committed. It was designed to be a low-commitment Church.

Jesus Christ asks us to commit our lives to him and demands everything of us. Commitment to his Church is sec-ondary. In many places today, the problem is that the Church demands everything of its members, and com-mitment to Jesus Christ is secondary.

The team wanted to make it easy for people to come to church. They wanted a low threshold for people to cross. You didn't have to sit quietly and behave in the right way and know what was going on, to come to this church.

You didn't have to believe in God to come to this church. Heavens above, it could even be a place where the unchurched encountered the Gospel!

The Upper Room is like a restaurant that has decided to cater for young people and give them what they want. It can be done. You can do it, too.

North Eastern Pease Pudding

1lb Whole dried peas (soaked overnight)
1 Onion, finely chopped   *2 Eggs*
2oz Butter   *Salt and pepper*

Rinse the peas until the water runs clear. Put them in a saucepan with the onion and cover with cold water. Bring to the boil, cover and simmer for two and a half hours.

In a large mixing bowl, beat the eggs and add the melted butter and salt and pepper to taste. Traditionally pease pudding has a *lot* of pepper.

The next bit has to be done quickly. Drain the peas using a colander. Then while they are still warm either mash them and add them to the egg and butter mixture and beat together, or add them to the egg and butter mixture and use a food processor to blend everything together.

The second option is a lot less work, but not traditional. The result should be a smooth yellowish paste.

Pease pudding can be served whilst hot, or allowed to cool and spread on sandwiches, or in the pot, nine days old.

Chapter 11
What happens next?

Putting it into practice

Put on that apron

Maybe you are reading this book because you are dissatisfied with church worship. If you are, then you are not alone. Millions never darken our door, and one of the reasons is the poverty of our worship.

Something needs to change, and you can change it. That change is needed urgently, but not every Church is ready. It is no good serving a delicious new menu, if the rest of the Church is quite satisfied with the traditional Sunday roast. They like it, and they can't see why anybody else does not like it.

If the people do not want to change, then it is going to be a slow and frustrating process in your church. But keep at it, and encourage people to try new things. You could even buy them a copy of this book to show them what could be done!

Where are these people?

Maybe you are reading this book because you have responsibility in a church and you want to see worship leaders in your congregation. Where can you find them, and how can you encourage them?

One way is to ask for volunteers. If there are others who feel like you do about worship, they may well come forward.

Another way is to provide opportunities for the congregation to be involved in your worship. *Involvement* is more than *participation*. It is not enough just to have the cooks preparing a course – they need to help in choosing the menu.

A third way of encouraging volunteers is not to put too many obstacles in the way of those wishing to lead worship. In many churches the leadership of worship is restricted to the educated few and new people are expected to go through a rigorous and academic training course.

I believe that when the Church trains worship-leaders, what it really does is train people to be 'churchy'. Instead of showing folk the joy of cooking and how to create new recipes, it pushes them into the pattern of providing traditional meals. Instead of letting them use their own language to describe the majesty of God, it pushes them into the pattern of using church language instead.

As a Church leader you should encourage people to use their own voices to praise God. You could use this book to design your own training course, or use this book in house groups so that the whole congregation could take part in the debate and *own* the worship.

Could I lead worship?

Maybe you are reading this book because somebody has asked you to do something. Perhaps you have been asked to speak in a house group, or to give the epilogue at a youth club or to take part in a prayer meeting.

Right now, you might be feeling a sense of your own inadequacy and how there are far better people than you to lead worship. If you feel like that, then congratulations – that is how the vast majority of leaders feel when they start out. When it comes to *Cooking up worship*, there will be times when you will feel that other cooks do the job far better than you ever can. There will be times when they feel the same about you.

If you are asked to be involved and people keep on asking you, even when you are not sure whether what you do is any good, then God could be using the people around you to call you to leadership. Instead of giving all the reasons why you *can't* lead worship, why not ask God to show you how you *can* lead worship?

The next step is actually to do something. Ask your Church leaders if you can be formally involved in leading worship. Make sure that you work within the rules, so that you can be helped to grow and develop. Most denominations have some kind of provision for this to happen. Otherwise they would never have any new leaders!

Seven former professions of famous people of God

- ☺ Fisherman:
  Simon, Andrew
- ☺ Tax collector:
  Matthew
- ☺ Woman of ill-repute (allegedly):
  Mary Magdalene
- ☺ Terrorist (allegedly):
  Simon the Zealot
- ☺ Persecutor of Christians:
  St Paul
- ☺ Captain of a slave ship:
  John Newton, writer of
  Amazing grace
- ☺ Watergate conspirator:
  Chuck Colson

You won't know if you should lead worship until you have tried. It is no use just talking about it. At some stage you are going to have to get down and do something about it. What is stopping you from responding today? You may feel the call of God, but think that it is for people better than you. Well, there is nobody better than you. The saints of God have not been the best qualified people; instead they have been the ones who said 'Yes' to God.

After reading this book, I hope that you can see that leading worship is not just for the important, or the loud, or the well-educated. *Anybody* can lead worship, because God has created us all with the ability to worship. That is what you are designed for.

The first disciples were ordinary men and women whose lives were touched by the Master, and who changed the history of the world by the power of the Holy Spirit. God can work in you as well.

God chooses whoever God wants to serve in the world. Who is to say that God is making the wrong choice?

The question you must answer now is not 'Can God work in me?' but instead 'Will I let God work in me?'

Only you know the answer to that question.

Stepping out

1. Wash your hands.

2. Switch on the oven.

3. Get cracking!

Chapter 12

In your larder ———————————

——————— Resources available to help you

Books on worship and music

Alpha Worship Set
Alpha Head Office,
Holy Trinity Brompton,
Brompton Road,
London SW7 1JA – www.alpha.org.uk

The Iona Community Worship Book
Wild Goose Publications, Unit 15,
Six Harmony Row,
Glasgow
G51 3BA – www.iona.org.uk

Songs and Prayers from Taizé
Geoffrey Chapman Mowbray,
Stanley House, 3 Fleets Lane,
Poole BH15 3AJ – www.taize.fr

The Ministers Manual 1998, 1999 etc.
ed James W Cox –
HarperSanFrancisco

The Worship Section online in
www.chrbook.com
CBD Christian Book Distributors

The Worship Section online in
www.amazon.co.uk
Amazon Booksellers

The Worship Section online in
www.cpas.org.uk
CPAS Anglican Mission Agency

The Worship Section online in
www.kevinmayhewltd.com
Kevin Mayhew Ltd, Publishers

Books on preaching

The Joy of Preaching
Phillips Brooks
Kregel Publications 08254 2276 0

To Preach or not to Preach
David C Norrington
Paternoster Press 085364 697 x

An Evangelical Theology of Preaching
Donald English
Abingdon Press 0687 121787

Books on prayer

Turn but a stone
Edmund Banyard
NCEC 07197 0785 4

Prayers for the Church Community
NCEC 07197 0205 4

Praying with the New Testament
Triangle 0281 04343 4

Thank God
Tony Jasper
Lion 085648 346 X

Books on the Bible

History of the Bible in English
F F Bruce
Lutterworth 07188 2662 0

Books with traditional approaches

Groundwork of Worship and Preaching
Richard Jones
Epworth 07162 0355 3

Introduction to Christian Worship
James White
Abingdon 0687 19509 8

Groundwork of Christian Worship
Susan J. White
Epworth 07162 0510 6

Books with different approaches

Rediscovering Church
Lynne & Bill Hybels
Zondervan 0310 59320 4

Starting a Seeker-Sensitive Service
Ed Dobson
Zondervan 0310 38481 8

Entertainment Evangelism
Walt Kallestad
Abingdon 0687 05450 8

'Kidz Klubs', The Alpha *of Children's Evangelism?*
Philip Clark & Geoff Pearson
Grove 1 85174 396 0

Christian drama

Rock Solid
Anne Collins
ISBN 1 84003 100 X

Direct Approach
Anne Collins
ISBN 1 84003 229 4

The Log in my Eye
Michael Catchpool and Pat Lunt
ISBN 1 84003 194 8

Say it, Act it!, Books 1 and 2
Michael Catchpool and Pat Lunt
ISBN 1 84003 377 0/

All from Kevin Mayhew Ltd, Buxhall, Stowmarket, Suffolk. IP14 3DJ
www.kevinmayhewltd.com

Addresses for children's/all-age material

Growing into Hope
Birmingham Initiative Christian Education,
Ladywood Methodist Church,
St Vincent Street West,
Birmingham B16 8RW

Living Stones, Years A, B and C
Susan Sayers
Come to the Feast, Books 1 and 2
Stuart Thomas

Both from Kevin Mayhew Ltd, Buxhall, Stowmarket, Suffolk IP14 3DJ –
www.kevinmayhewltd.com

Partners in Learning
Methodist Publishing House,
20 Ivatt Way,
Peterborough PE3 7PG

S.A.L.T. (Sharing And Learning Together)
Scripture Union
Box No 764, Oxford OX4 5FG
www.scripture.org.uk

Address of copyright agency

Christian Copyright Licensing
(Europe) Ltd
PO Box 1339,
Eastbourne
East Sussex BN21 4SA
www.ccli.com